GREAT TASTES

30 MINUTE MEALS

First published in 2010 by Bay Books, an imprint of Murdoch Books Pty Limited

Murdoch Books Australia
Pier 8/9
23 Hickson Road
Millers Point NSW 2000
Phone: +61 (0) 2 8220 2000
Fax: +61 (0) 2 8220 2558
www.murdochbooks.com.au

Murdoch Books UK Limited
Erico House, 6th Floor
93–99 Upper Richmond Road
Putney, London SW15 2TG
Phone: +44 (0) 20 8785 5995
Fax: +44 (0) 20 8785 5985
www.murdochbooks.co.uk

Chief Executive: Juliet Rogers
Publishing Director: Kay Scarlett
Publisher: Lynn Lewis
Senior Designer: Heather Menzies
Design Team: Transformer Creative
Production: Kita George

ISBN: 9781741968736

PRINTED IN CHINA

OVEN GUIDE: You may find cooking times vary depending on the oven you are using. For fan-forced ovens, as a general rule, set the oven temperature to 20°C (35°F) lower than indicated in the recipe.

GREAT TASTES

30 MINUTE MEALS

More than 120 easy recipes for every day

bay books

CONTENTS

KITCHEN EQUIPMENT

Saving time in the kitchen involves reliable recipes, an organized way of working and the appropriate utensils for the job in hand. Buy the best quality items that you can afford and build up your collection over time.

Basic knives

Kitchen knives Buy the best you can afford. Make sure they are comfortable to hold and the handle and blade are well balanced. Put them in a block to keep them sharp — if they bash around against things in a drawer they will blunt quickly. You will need one large knife for chopping, one medium knife and one small serrated knife for fruit and tomatoes — go for one with a pointed end that will easily pierce the skins. A serrated bread knife is used for slicing loaves. A flat-bladed knife is not a good substitute as it squashes the loaf rather than cuts it. Use a steel to keep all your knife edges sharp, and sharpen before every use.

Scissors Kitchen scissors should have tough blades, preferably with a serrated edge. The lower handle should be large enough to grip with three fingers. Poultry shears have a cutting point near the pivot for gripping bones as you cut them.

Specialist knives

Specialist knives These are needed if you plan on being more adventurous with your cooking. A **mezzaluna** is a double-handled knife with one or two curved blades, which are rocked from side to side to chop herbs. The word means 'half moon'. An **oyster knife** is essential for opening oysters and other shellfish. Its short, flat blade with two cutting edges slides easily between shells. For basic meat preparation, a **boning knife** with a very strong, thin blade will help. A **citrus zester** and **canelle knife** easily peel off zest in thin or thick shreds using a row of small holes or a deeper, V-shaped cutting edge.

Saucepans and frying pans

Saucepans These should be always good quality and the most expensive ones that you can afford. There is a huge range on the market but stainless steel with a sandwich base (stainless steel sandwiching a metal such as copper that conducts heat well) are a good bet for even heat distribution. Stainless steel is also non-reactive (it will not be affected by the use of an acid such as lemon juice). Choose pans with comfortable handles (check these do not heat up) and lids that have a tight seal. You will need one large pan and a couple of smaller ones. A pasta boiler with a fitted drainer is useful for cooking pasta. **Frying pans** Like saucepans, these should be good quality. Cast-iron ones are heavy but last a long time. Non-stick ones have to be used with wooden or plastic implements. An ovenproof handle is useful for making anything that needs to be finished in the oven or under a grill (broiler).

Ovenware

Ovenware These should be good quality and be able to be used on the stovetop and in the oven. Casseroles need to be heavy enough to absorb and retain heat and also need tight-fitting lids so as not to let any moisture escape. Cast-iron or enamelled ones (with cast-iron or steel underneath) are generally the best as they conduct heat well. You will need several sizes as it is important that the recipe fits the casserole. Baking and gratin dishes should be fully ovenproof and able to withstand high heat. Enamel, cast-iron and stoneware are good options.

Roasting tin This should be made from stainless steel or from anodized aluminium so the tins can be used over a heat source without buckling. One with a rack is particularly useful so that meat and poultry can be roasted and the fat and juices easily collected underneath.

General equipment

Chopping board An essential piece of equipment, whether wooden or polyethylene. Whichever you choose, your board should be kept spotlessly clean.

Graters These vary in shape, but the important part is the cutting edge, which should be very sharp. A box grater doesn't slip easily and is good for large quantities.

Kitchen knives

Saucepans

Enamelled casseroles

Box graters

Potato masher Potato mashers work on all cooked vegetables. Old-style mashers with a cut grid often work better.

Tin opener It is worth buying a good-quality one that grips properly and fits comfortably in your hand.

Lemon squeezer Available in glass, ceramic, plastic and wood. The squeezers with a container underneath for collecting the juice are the most useful.

Sieves These come in a range of sizes. Larger colanders are best for draining. Round-bottomed stainless steel sieves have a mesh suitable for sifting and puréeing and nylon mesh sieves are for fine sifting and puréeing.

Kitchen utensils

Spoons Useful for stirring, mixing and beating. Wooden spoons are good because they do not conduct heat, do not scratch and are non-reactive. Metal spoons are used for folding ingredients. A perforated spoon is useful for draining. Ladles are made for serving liquids.

Pastry brush Made with either nylon or natural bristles and can be flat or round.

Peeler A good peeler shaves only a thin skin off vegetables.

Rubber spatula This can scrape a bowl completely clean.

Fish slice This needs enough flexibility to be able to slide under things easily.

Asian equipment

Wok Buy a carbon steel or pressed steel wok from your local Chinatown as they conduct heat better. Season by rubbing it with salt and hot oil, then wipe it out after each use rather than washing it — this will build up a non-stick surface over time. Use with a wok charn for stir-frying. This is a shovel-like spatula ideal for tossing food around the curved side of the wok.

Chopper/cleaver These are used for chopping through bones, as well as an all-purpose knife. Buy a good heavy one for chopping and a lighter one for slicing.

Metal or bamboo tongs Very useful for turning things over, or lifting things out of boiling liquids.

Clay pot Glazed on the inside and used for slow cooking as it heats up evenly all over.

Steamers Bamboo stackable steamers allow food to be cooked in steam.

Specialist equipment

Mortar and pestle A bowl (mortar) with a slightly rough surface and a crushing stick (pestle) that fits the curvature of the bowl and provides the second grinding surface. Very good for crushing seeds, spices and cloves of garlic.

Salt and pepper mills (grinders) Buy a pepper mill with a steel grinding mechanism for efficiency and an adjustable grind.

Scales, measuring cups and thermometers

Scales You need only one good-quality set of scales. Choose one with both metric and imperial weights.

Measuring jugs Plastic and glass jugs are best to use as you can read them easily. Be sure to choose one with the calibrations clearly visible.

Measuring cups Often used instead of scales for dry and liquid measures. Available in fractions and multiples of cup measures.

Measuring spoons Available in sets ranging from ¼ teaspoon to 1 tablespoon. Dry measurements should be levelled off with a knife to be accurate.

Thermometers These are an essential item for accurate oil measurements. An oven thermometer is used to ensure that the thermostat is registering accurately. These are important to ensure good results.

Wooden spoons

Bamboo steamer

Mortar and pestle

Metal measuring cups

PASTA, RICE & NOODLES

SPAGHETTI PUTTANESCA

SERVES 4

400 g (14 oz) spaghetti

2 tablespoons olive oil

1 onion, finely chopped

2 garlic cloves, finely sliced

1 small red chilli, cored, seeded
and sliced

6 anchovy fillets, finely chopped

400 g (14 oz) tinned chopped tomatoes

1 tablespoon fresh oregano,
finely chopped

16 black olives, halved and pitted

2 tablespoons baby capers

1 handful basil leaves

1 Cook the pasta in a large saucepan of boiling salted water until al dente. Drain well and return to the pan to keep warm.

2 Meanwhile, heat the olive oil in a large saucepan and add the onion, garlic and chilli. Gently fry for about 8 minutes, or until the onion is soft. Add the anchovies and cook for a further 1 minute.

3 Add the tomato, oregano, olive halves and capers and bring to the boil. Reduce the heat, season with salt and pepper, and leave the sauce to simmer for 3 minutes.

4 Add the spaghetti to the sauce. Toss together well so that the pasta is coated in the sauce. Scatter the basil over the top.

PENNE ALL'ARRABBIATA

SERVES 4

400 g (14 oz) penne

2 large garlic cloves, thinly sliced

1–2 dried chillies

800 g (1 lb 12 oz) tinned tomatoes

2 tablespoons olive oil

1 basil sprig, torn into pieces

1   Cook the pasta in a large saucepan of boiling salted water until al dente. Drain well and return to the pan to keep warm.

2   Meanwhile, heat the olive oil in a saucepan over low heat. Add the garlic and chillies, turning the chillies over during cooking. Add the tomatoes and season. Cook, breaking up the tomatoes with a wooden spoon, for about 20 minutes, or until thick.

3   Add the basil to the sauce and toss with the pasta. Season to taste.

PENNE CARBONARA

SERVES 4–6

400 g (14 oz) penne

1 tablespoon olive oil

200 g (7 oz) piece pancetta or bacon, cut into long thin strips

6 egg yolks

185 ml (6 fl oz/¾ cup) pouring cream

75 g (2½ oz/¾ cup) grated parmesan cheese

1 **Cook the pasta** in a large saucepan of boiling salted water until al dente. Drain well and return to the pan to keep warm.

2 **Meanwhile,** heat the oil in a frying pan over high heat. Cook the pancetta for about 6 minutes, or until crisp and golden. Remove with a slotted spoon and drain well on paper towel.

3 **Beat the egg yolks,** cream and parmesan together in a bowl and season well.

4 **Pour the egg mixture** over the pasta, tossing gently. Add the pancetta and cook over very low heat for 30–60 seconds, or until the sauce thickens and coats the pasta. Season and serve immediately.

Note: Be careful not to cook the pasta over high heat once you have added the egg mixture, or the sauce risks being scrambled by the heat.

CREAMY BOSCAIOLA

SERVES 4

500 g (1 lb 2 oz) pasta

1 tablespoon olive oil

6 bacon slices, chopped

200 g (7 oz) button mushrooms, sliced

625 ml (21½ fl oz/2½ cups) pouring cream

2 spring onions (scallions), sliced

1 tablespoon chopped flat-leaf (Italian) parsley

1   Cook the pasta in a large saucepan of boiling salted water until al dente. Drain well and return to the pan to keep warm.

2   While the pasta is cooking, heat the oil in a large frying pan, add the bacon and mushroom and cook, stirring, for 5 minutes, or until golden brown.

3   Stir in a little of the cream and scrape the wooden spoon on the bottom of the pan to dislodge any bacon that has stuck.

4   Add the remaining cream, bring to the boil and cook over high heat for 15 minutes, or until the sauce is thick enough to coat the back of a spoon. Stir the spring onion through the mixture. Pour the sauce over the pasta and toss to combine. Serve sprinkled with the parsley.

Note: This sauce is normally served with spaghetti, but you can use any pasta. We have shown it with pappardelle.

CHICKEN RAVIOLI WITH PESTO

SERVES 4

625 g (1 lb 6 oz) chicken ravioli

50 g (2 oz) basil

2 garlic cloves

40 g (1½ oz/¼ cup) pine nuts, toasted

125 ml (4 fl oz/½ cup) extra virgin
olive oil

50 g (2 oz/½ cup) grated parmesan
cheese

50 g (1¾ oz) pecorino cheese, grated

15 g (½ oz) basil, extra, torn

30 g (1 oz) shaved parmesan cheese,
to serve

1 **Cook the pasta** in a large saucepan of boiling salted water until al dente. Drain well and return to the pan to keep warm.

2 **Meanwhile,** blend the basil, garlic, pine nuts and olive oil in a food processor or blender until smooth.

3 **Stir in the grated parmesan** and pecorino and season to taste with salt and pepper.

4 **Drain the pasta,** reserving 1 tablespoon of the cooking water to add to the pesto. Carefully toss the ravioli in the pesto and reserved water.

5 **To serve,** drizzle with the extra virgin olive oil and top with a little torn basil and the cheeses.

PENNE ALLA NAPOLITANA

SERVES 4–6

2 tablespoons olive oil
1 onion, finely chopped
2–3 garlic cloves, finely chopped
1 small carrot, finely diced
1 celery stalk, finely diced
800 g (1 lb 12 oz) tinned peeled, chopped tomatoes or 1 kg (2 lb 4 oz) ripe tomatoes, peeled and chopped
1 tablespoon tomato paste (concentrated purée)
3 tablespoons shredded basil
500 g (1 lb 2 oz) penne
freshly grated parmesan cheese, to serve (optional)

1 Heat the oil in a large frying pan. Add the onion and garlic and cook for 2 minutes, or until golden. Add the carrot and celery and cook for a further 2 minutes.

2 Add tomato and tomato paste. Simmer for 20 minutes, or until the sauce thickens, stirring occasionally. Stir in the shredded basil and season to taste.

3 While the sauce is cooking, cook the pasta in a large saucepan of rapidly boiling salted water until al dente. Drain well and return to the pan.

4 Add the sauce to the pasta and mix well. Serve with freshly grated parmesan cheese, if desired.

PASTA WITH CREAMY SEMI-DRIED TOMATO SAUCE

SERVES 4

4 bacon slices

625 g (1 lb 6 oz) veal or chicken agnolotti

1 tablespoon olive oil

2 garlic cloves, finely chopped

110 g (4 oz/⅔ cup) thinly sliced semi-dried (sun-blushed) tomatoes

1 tablespoon chopped thyme

375 ml (13 fl oz/1½ cups) cream

1 teaspoon finely grated lemon zest

35 g (1 oz/⅓ cup) finely grated parmesan cheese

1   Grill (broil) the bacon for 5 minutes each side, or until crisp and golden. Remove, drain well on paper towel, then break into pieces.

2   Cook the pasta in a large saucepan of boiling salted water until al dente. Drain well and return to the pan to keep warm.

3   Heat the oil in a frying pan and cook the garlic over medium heat for 1 minute, or until just golden. Add the tomato and thyme and cook for 1 minute.

4   Add the cream, bring to the boil, then reduce the heat and simmer for 6–8 minutes, or until the cream has thickened and reduced by one third. Season, add the lemon zest, and 2 tablespoons of the parmesan.

5   Add the pasta to the sauce and stir gently to combine. Sprinkle with the remaining parmesan and the bacon pieces.

LINGUINE PESTO

SERVES 4–6

PESTO

100 g (4 oz) basil

2 garlic cloves, crushed

40 g (1½ oz/¼ cup) pine nuts, toasted

185 ml (6 fl oz/¾ cup) olive oil

50 g (2 oz/½ cup) freshly grated
  parmesan cheese, plus extra, to serve

500 g (1 lb 2 oz) linguine

1 **To make the pesto,** process the basil, garlic and pine nuts together in a food processor. With the motor running, add the oil in a steady stream until mixed to a smooth paste.

2 **Transfer the mixture** to a bowl, stir in the parmesan cheese and season to taste.

3 **Cook the pasta** in a large saucepan of boiling salted water until al dente. Drain well and return to the pan to keep warm.

4 **Toss enough of the pesto** through the pasta to coat well. Serve sprinkled with parmesan.

Note: Refrigerate any leftover pesto in an airtight jar for up to a week. Cover the surface with a layer of oil. Freeze for up to 1 month.

TAGLIATELLE WITH SALMON AND CREAMY DILL DRESSING

SERVES 4

350 g (12 oz) fresh tagliatelle

3 tablespoons olive oil

3 x 200 g (7 oz) salmon fillets, skinned and boned (ask your fishmonger to do this for you)

3 garlic cloves, crushed

375 ml (13 fl oz/1½ cups) cream

1½ tablespoons chopped dill

1 teaspoon mustard powder

1 tablespoon lemon juice

40 g (1½ oz) shaved parmesan cheese

1 **Cook the pasta** in a large saucepan of boiling water until al dente. Drain, then toss with 1 tablespoon oil.

2 **Meanwhile,** heat the remaining oil in a deep frying pan; cook the salmon for 2 minutes each side, or until crisp on the outside but still pink inside. Remove from the pan, cut into 2 cm (¾ in) cubes.

3 **In the same pan,** add the garlic and cook for 30 seconds, or until fragrant. Add the cream, dill and mustard powder, bring to the boil, then reduce the heat and simmer, stirring, for 4–5 minutes, or until thickened. Season.

4 **Add the salmon** and any juices plus the lemon juice to the dill sauce and stir until warm. Gently toss the salmon sauce through the pasta and divide among four serving bowls. Sprinkle with parmesan and serve.

TAGLIATELLE WITH VEAL, WINE AND CREAM

SERVES 4

500 g (1 lb 2 oz) veal scaloppine or escalopes, cut into thin strips
plain (all-purpose) flour, seasoned
60 g (2 oz) butter
1 onion, sliced
125 ml (4 fl oz/½ cup) dry white wine
60 ml (2 fl oz/¼ cup) beef stock or chicken stock
170 ml (6 fl oz/⅔ cup) pouring cream
600 g (1 lb 5 oz) fresh plain or spinach tagliatelle (or a mixture of both)
1 tablespoon freshly grated parmesan cheese, plus extra, to serve (optional)
flat-leaf (Italian) parsley, to garnish

1 **Coat the veal strips** with the seasoned flour. Melt the butter in a frying pan. Add the veal strips and fry quickly until browned. Remove with a slotted spoon and set aside.

2 **Add the onion slices** to the pan and stir until soft and golden. Pour in the wine and cook rapidly to reduce the liquid. Add the stock and cream and season to taste. Reduce the sauce again, and add the veal towards the end.

3 **Meanwhile,** cook the tagliatelle in a large saucepan of rapidly boiling salted water until al dente. Drain and transfer to a warm serving dish.

4 **Stir the parmesan** through the sauce. Pour the sauce over the pasta. Serve with extra parmesan, if desired, and garnish with flat-leaf parsley.

SPICY EGGPLANT SPAGHETTI

SERVES 4

300 g (11 oz) spaghetti

125 ml (4 fl oz/½ cup) extra virgin olive oil

2 red chillies, finely sliced

1 onion, finely chopped

3 garlic cloves, crushed

4 bacon slices, chopped

400 g (14 oz) eggplant (aubergine), diced

2 tablespoons balsamic vinegar

2 tomatoes, chopped

3 tablespoons shredded basil

1 **Cook the pasta** in a large saucepan of boiling salted water until al dente. Drain well and return to the pan to keep warm.

2 **Heat 1 tablespoon of the oil** in a large, deep frying pan over medium heat. Cook the chilli, onion, garlic and bacon for about 5 minutes, or until the onion is golden and the bacon browned. Remove from the pan and set aside.

3 **Add half the remaining oil** to the pan and cook half the eggplant over high heat, tossing to brown on all sides. Remove from the pan and set aside to keep warm. Repeat with the remaining oil and eggplant. Return the bacon mixture and all the eggplant to the pan. Add the vinegar, tomato and basil and cook until heated through. Season well.

4 **Serve the spaghetti** topped with the eggplant mixture.

PASTA GNOCCHI WITH GRILLED CAPSICUM

SERVES 4–6

6 large red capsicums (peppers), halved
400 g (14 oz) pasta gnocchi (see Note)
2 tablespoons olive oil
1 onion, thinly sliced
3 garlic cloves, finely chopped
2 tablespoons shredded basil leaves
whole basil leaves, to garnish
shaved parmesan cheese, to serve

1 **Cut the capsicums** into large flattish pieces. Cook, skin side up, under a hot grill (broiler) until the skin blackens and blisters. Cool in a plastic bag, then peel the skin.

2 **Cook the pasta** in a large saucepan of boiling salted water until al dente. Drain well and return to the pan to keep warm.

3 **Meanwhile,** heat the oil in a large frying pan, add the onion and garlic and cook over medium heat for 5 minutes, or until soft. Slice 1 capsicum into thin strips and add to the onion mixture.

4 **Chop the remaining capsicum,** then purée in a food processor until smooth. Add to the onion mixture and cook over low heat for 5 minutes, or until warmed through.

5 **Toss together the sauce** and pasta. Season, then stir in the shredded basil. Garnish with the basil leaves and serve with shaved parmesan cheese.

Note: Pasta gnocchi is similar in shape to potato gnocchi. If unavailable, use conchiglie or orecchiette.

PENNE WITH MUSHROOM AND HERB SAUCE

SERVES 4

2 tablespoons olive oil

500 g (1 lb 2 oz) button mushrooms, sliced

2 garlic cloves, crushed

2 teaspoons chopped marjoram

125 ml (4 fl oz/½ cup) dry white wine

4 tablespoons pouring cream

375 g (13 oz) penne

1 tablespoon lemon juice

1 teaspoon finely grated lemon zest

2 tablespoons chopped flat-leaf (Italian) parsley

50 g (2 oz/½ cup) grated parmesan cheese

1 Heat the oil in a large heavy-based frying pan over high heat. Add the mushrooms and cook for 3 minutes, stirring constantly to prevent the mushrooms from burning.

2 Add the garlic and marjoram and cook for a further 2 minutes. Add the white wine to the pan, reduce the heat and simmer for 5 minutes or until nearly all the liquid has evaporated. Stir in the cream and cook over low heat for 5 minutes, or until thick.

3 Cook the pasta in a saucepan of boiling salted water until al dente. Drain well and return to the pan to keep warm.

4 Add the lemon juice, zest, parsley and half the parmesan to the sauce. Season to taste. Toss the pasta through the sauce and sprinkle with the remaining parmesan.

TUSCAN WARM PASTA SALAD

SERVES 6

500 g (1 lb 2 oz) rigatoni
80 ml (3 fl oz/⅓ cup) olive oil
1 garlic clove, crushed
1 tablespoon balsamic vinegar
425 g (15 oz) tinned artichoke hearts, drained and quartered
8 thin prosciutto slices, chopped
80 g (3 oz/½ cup) sun-dried (sun-blushed) tomatoes in oil, drained and thinly sliced
4 tablespoons basil, shredded
70 g (2 oz) rocket (arugula) leaves, washed and drained well
40 g (1½ oz/¼ cup) pine nuts, toasted
45 g (1½ oz/¼ cup) black Italian olives

1 Add the rigatoni to a large saucepan of rapidly boiling water and cook until al dente. Drain the pasta thoroughly and transfer to a large bowl.

2 While the pasta is cooking, whisk together the oil, garlic and balsamic vinegar. Toss the dressing through the hot pasta. Allow the pasta to cool slightly. Add the artichoke hearts, prosciutto, sun-dried tomato, basil, rocket, pine nuts and olives.

3 Toss all the ingredients together until well combined. Season to taste.

Note: To toast the pine nuts, cook in a dry frying pan over medium heat for 1–2 minutes, until lightly golden. Take care that they do not burn. Allow to cool.

RAVIOLI WITH ROASTED RED CAPSICUM SAUCE

SERVES 4

6 red capsicums (peppers)

625 g (1 lb 6 oz) ravioli

2 tablespoons olive oil

3 garlic cloves, crushed

2 leeks, thinly sliced

1 tablespoon chopped oregano

2 teaspoons soft brown sugar

250 ml (9 fl oz/1 cup) vegetable or chicken stock

1 **Cut the capsicum** into large flattish pieces and remove the membrane and seeds. Cook, skin side up, under a hot grill (broiler) until the skin blackens and blisters. Cool in a plastic bag, then peel the skin.

2 **Cook the pasta** in a large saucepan of boiling salted water until al dente. Drain well and return to the pan to keep warm

3 **Meanwhile,** heat the olive oil in a frying pan over medium heat. Cook the garlic and leek for 3–4 minutes, or until softened. Add the oregano and brown sugar and stir for 1 minute.

4 **Place the capsicum** and leek mixture in a food processor or blender, season and process until combined. Add the stock and process until smooth. Gently toss the sauce through the pasta over low heat until warmed through.

PENNE WITH BACON, RICOTTA CHEESE AND BASIL SAUCE

SERVES 4

2 teaspoons olive oil

4 bacon slices, chopped

2–3 garlic cloves, crushed

1 onion, finely chopped

2 spring onions (scallions), finely chopped

250 g (9 oz/1 cup) low-fat ricotta cheese

3 handfuls basil, finely chopped, plus extra whole leaves, to garnish

325 g (11 oz) penne

12 cherry tomatoes, halved

1 Heat the oil in a frying pan. Add the bacon, garlic, onion and spring onion and stir over medium heat for 5 minutes, or until cooked. Remove from the heat, stir in the ricotta and chopped basil and beat until smooth.

2 Cook the pasta in a large saucepan of boiling salted water for 10 minutes, or until al dente. Just prior to draining pasta, add about 250 ml (9 fl oz/1 cup) of the pasta cooking water to the ricotta mixture to thin the sauce. Add a little more water if you prefer an even thinner sauce. Season with salt and freshly ground black pepper.

3 Drain the pasta and stir the ricotta sauce and tomato halves through the pasta. Garnish with extra basil.

SPAGHETTI VONGOLE

SERVES 4

1 kg (2 lb 4 oz) baby clams (vongole)

375 g (13 oz) spaghetti

125 ml (4 fl oz/½ cup) extra virgin olive oil

40 g (1½ oz) butter

1 small onion, very finely chopped

6 large garlic cloves, finely chopped

125 ml (4 fl oz/½ cup) dry white wine

1 small red chilli, seeded and finely chopped

3 tablespoons chopped flat-leaf (Italian) parsley

1   Scrub the clams with a small stiff brush to remove any grit, discarding any that are open or cracked. Soak and rinse the clams in several changes of water over 1 hour, or until the water is clean and free of grit. Drain and set aside.

2   Cook the pasta in a large saucepan of boiling salted water until al dente. Drain well and return to the pan to keep warm.

3   Heat the oil and 1 tablespoon of the butter in a large saucepan over medium heat. Add the onion and half the garlic and cook for 10 minutes, or until lightly golden.

4   Add wine and cook for 2 minutes. Add the clams, chilli and the remaining butter and garlic. Cook, covered, for 8 minutes, shaking regularly, until the clams pop open. Discard any that are still closed.

5   Stir in parsley and season. Add pasta and toss together.

SUMMER SEAFOOD MARINARA

SERVES 4

300 g (11 oz) fresh saffron angel hair pasta

1 tablespoon extra virgin olive oil

30 g (1 oz) butter

2 garlic cloves, finely chopped

1 large onion, finely chopped

1 small red chilli, finely chopped

600 g (1 lb 5 oz) tinned peeled tomatoes, chopped

250 ml (9 fl oz/1 cup) white wine

zest of 1 lemon

½ tablespoon sugar

200 g (7 oz) scallops without roe

500 g (1 lb 2 oz) raw prawns (shrimp), peeled and deveined

300 g (11 oz) clams (vongole)

1 **Cook the pasta** in a large saucepan of boiling salted water until al dente. Drain well and return to the pan to keep warm.

2 **Meanwhile,** heat the oil and butter in a frying pan over medium heat. Add the garlic, onion and chilli and cook for 5 minutes, or until soft. Add the tomatoes and wine and bring to the boil. Cook for 10 minutes, or until the sauce has thickened slightly.

3 **Add the lemon zest,** sugar, scallops, prawns and clams. Cook, covered, for 5 minutes, or until the seafood is tender. Discard any clams that do not open. Season and serve the pasta topped with the sauce.

MEATBALLS WITH FUSILLI

SERVES 4

750 g (1 lb 10 oz) minced (ground) pork and veal

80 g (3 oz/1 cup) fresh breadcrumbs

3 tablespoons freshly grated parmesan cheese

1 onion, finely chopped

2 tablespoons chopped flat-leaf (Italian) parsley

1 egg, beaten

1 garlic clove, crushed

zest and juice of ½ lemon

30 g (1 oz/¼ cup) plain (all-purpose) flour, seasoned

2 tablespoons olive oil

500 g (1 lb 2 oz) fusilli

SAUCE

425 g (15 oz) tinned tomato passata (puréed tomatoes)

125 ml (4 fl oz/½ cup) beef stock

125 ml (4 fl oz/½ cup) red wine

2 tablespoons chopped basil

1 garlic clove, crushed

1 Combine the meat, breadcrumbs, parmesan, onion, parsley, egg, garlic, lemon zest and juice in a large bowl and season to taste.

2 Roll tablespoons of the mixture into balls and roll the balls in the seasoned flour.

3 Heat the oil in a large frying pan and fry the meatballs until golden. Remove from the pan and drain well on paper towels. Remove the excess fat and meat juices from the pan.

4 To make the sauce, in the same pan, combine the tomato passata, stock, wine, basil, garlic, salt and pepper. Bring to the boil.

5 Reduce the heat and return the meatballs to the pan. Allow to simmer for 10–15 minutes.

6 Meanwhile, cook the pasta in a saucepan of boiling salted water until al dente. Drain well and serve with meatballs and sauce over the top.

HERB-FILLED RAVIOLI WITH SAGE BUTTER

BUTTER PASTA

300 g (11 oz) plain (all-purpose) flour

3 eggs, beaten

60 ml (2 fl oz/¼ cup) olive oil

250 g (9 oz/1 cup) ricotta cheese

2 tablespoons freshly grated parmesan cheese, plus extra, shaved, to garnish

2 teaspoons snipped chives

1 tablespoon chopped flat-leaf (Italian) parsley

2 teaspoons chopped basil

1 teaspoon chopped thyme

SAGE BUTTER

200 g (7 oz) butter

12 sage leaves

1 Sift the flour into a bowl and make a well in the centre. Gradually mix in eggs and oil. Turn out onto a lightly floured surface and knead for about 6 minutes, or until smooth. Cover with plastic wrap and leave for 30 minutes.

2 Combine the ricotta, parmesan and herbs. Season.

3 Divide the dough into four even portions. Lightly flour a large work surface and using a floured long rolling pin, roll out one portion from the centre to the edge. Continue, always rolling from in front of you outwards. Rotate the dough often. Fold the dough in half and roll it out again. Continue the process seven times to make a smooth circle of pasta about 5 mm (¼ inch) thick. Roll this sheet out quickly and smoothly to half the original thickness. Make four sheets of pasta, two slightly larger than the others. Cover with a tea towel (dish towel) to prevent drying out.

4 Place one of the smaller sheets on a work surface and place heaped teaspoons of filling at 5 cm (2 inch) intervals. Brush a little water between the filling along cutting lines. Top with a larger sheet. Firmly press the sheets together along the cutting lines. Cut ravioli along lines and transfer to a lightly floured baking tray. Repeat with remaining dough and filling.

5 Melt the butter over low heat in a small heavy-based pan, without stirring or shaking. Carefully pour the clear butter into another container. Discard the white sediment. Return clarified butter to a clean pan. Heat gently. Add sage and cook until crisp, not brown. Drain on paper towels. Reserve warm butter.

6 Cook the ravioli in batches in a large saucepan of salted simmering water for 6 minutes, or until tender. The water must not be boiling or the squares will split. Serve topped with warm sage butter and leaves. Garnish with the parmesan.

CHINESE FRIED RICE

SERVES 4

350 g (12 oz/1¾ cups) long-grain rice

1 tablespoon vegetable or peanut oil

2 eggs, beaten

3 Chinese sausages (lap cheong), thinly sliced on diagonal (see Note)

100 g (4 oz) snake (yard long) beans, cut into 2 cm (¾ inch) lengths

6 spring onions (scallions), finely chopped

2 garlic cloves, crushed

2 teaspoons grated fresh ginger

160 g (6 oz) small green prawns (shrimp), peeled and deveined

100 g (4 oz/⅔ cup) frozen peas, thawed

2 tablespoons soy sauce

2 spring onions (scallions), extra, thinly sliced on diagonal, to serve

1　**Wash the rice** under cold running water until the water runs clear. Bring a large saucepan of water to the boil, add the rice and cook for 10–12 minutes, or until tender. Drain and rinse under cold water to remove any excess starch. Spread out on a flat tray and refrigerate for 2 hours or overnight.

2　**Heat a wok** over high heat, add half the oil and swirl to coat. Add the egg, swirling to coat the side of the wok. When the egg is almost set, roll it up in the wok, turn the heat off, then remove. Roughly chop and set aside.

3　**Reheat the wok** over high heat, add the remaining oil and swirl to coat. Add the Chinese sausage and snake beans and stir-fry for 2–3 minutes. Add the spring onion, garlic and ginger and stir-fry for 1 minute. Add the prawns and stir-fry for 1–2 minutes, or until cooked. Stir in the rice and peas and toss until well combined and heated through. Stir in the soy sauce and serve garnished with the chopped egg and extra spring onion.

Note: Lap cheong sausage is a Chinese dried pork sausage and can be found in Asian food stores.

THAI BASIL FRIED RICE

SERVES 4

2 tablespoons oil

3 Asian shallots, sliced

1 garlic clove, finely chopped

1 small red chilli, finely chopped

100 g (4 oz) snake (yard long) or green beans, cut into short pieces

1 small red capsicum (pepper), cut into batons

90 g (3 oz) button mushrooms, halved

470 g (1 lb/2½ cups) cooked jasmine rice

1 teaspoon grated palm sugar (jaggery)

3 tablespoons light soy sauce

10 g (½ oz) Thai basil, shredded

1 tablespoon chopped coriander (cilantro) leaves

fried red Asian shallot flakes, to garnish

Thai basil leaves, to garnish

1 Heat a wok over high heat, add the oil and swirl. Stir-fry the shallots, garlic and chilli for 3 minutes, or until the shallots start to brown.

2 Add the beans, capsicum and mushrooms, stir-fry for 3 minutes, or until cooked, then stir in the cooked jasmine rice and heat through.

3 Dissolve the palm sugar in the soy sauce, then pour over the rice. Stir in the herbs. Garnish with the shallot flakes and basil.

CHICKEN PILAF

SERVES 6

½ large barbecued chicken

50 g (2 oz) margarine

1 onion, finely chopped

2 garlic cloves, crushed

300 g (11 oz/1½ cups) basmati rice

1 tablespoon currants

2 tablespoons finely chopped dried
  apricots

1 teaspoon ground cinnamon

pinch of ground cardamom

750 ml (26 fl oz/3 cups) chicken stock

1 handful coriander (cilantro) leaves,
  chopped

1 **Remove the skin** and any fat from the chicken and shred the meat into bite-sized pieces.

2 **Melt the margarine** in a large, deep frying pan over medium heat. Add the onion and garlic and cook for 2 minutes, stirring often. Add the rice, currants, apricots and spices and stir until well coated.

3 **Pour in the stock** and bring to the boil. Reduce the heat to low and simmer, covered, for about 15 minutes. Add a little water if the pilaf starts to dry out.

4 **Add the shredded chicken** and stir for about 1–2 minutes, or until thoroughly heated through. Stir in the coriander and serve immediately.

NASI GORENG

2 eggs

4 tablespoons oil

3 garlic cloves, finely chopped

1 onion, finely chopped

2 red chillies, seeded and very finely chopped

1 teaspoon shrimp paste

1 teaspoon coriander seeds

½ teaspoon sugar

400 g (14 oz) raw prawns (shrimp), peeled and deveined

200 g (7 oz) rump steak, thinly sliced

200 g (7 oz/1 cup) long-grain rice, cooked and cooled

2 teaspoons kecap manis

1 tablespoon soy sauce

4 spring onions (scallions), finely chopped

½ lettuce, finely shredded

1 cucumber, thinly sliced

3 tablespoons crisp fried onion

1 Beat the eggs and ¼ teaspoon salt together. Heat a frying pan over medium heat.

2 Pour about one-quarter of the egg into the pan and cook for 1–2 minutes, or until the omelette sets. Turn the omelette over and cook the other side for about 30 seconds. Remove from the pan and repeat with the remaining egg mixture, working with one-quarter of the egg mixture at a time. Allow to cool, then roll up and cut into strips.

3 Combine the garlic, onion, chilli, shrimp paste, coriander and sugar in a food processor or mortar and pestle, and process or pound to form a smooth paste.

4 Heat 1–2 tablespoons of the oil in a wok or large, deep frying pan. Add paste and cook over high heat for 1 minute, or until fragrant. Add the prawns and steak and stir-fry for about 3 minutes, or until they change colour.

5 Add the remaining oil and the cold rice to the wok and stir-fry, breaking up any lumps, until the rice is heated through. Add the kecap manis, soy sauce and spring onion and stir-fry for another minute.

6 Arrange the lettuce around the outside of a large platter. Put the rice in the centre and garnish with the omelette strips, cucumber slices and fried onion. Serve immediately.

BIRYANI-STYLE RICE

SERVES 4

200 g (7 oz/1 cup) basmati rice

pinch of saffron threads

1 cinnamon stick

4 cardamom pods, smashed

1 large potato, cut into 2 cm (¾ inch) cubes

1 teaspoon sea salt

3 tablespoons vegetable or peanut oil

1 eggplant (aubergine), cut into 2 cm (¾ inch) cubes

1 red onion, cut into thin wedges

3 garlic cloves, crushed

1 tablespoon grated fresh ginger

1 teaspoon dried chilli flakes

1 teaspoon ground cinnamon

1 teaspoon ground coriander

2 teaspoons ground cumin

1 teaspoon ground cardamom

1 teaspoon fennel seeds, ground

155 g (6 oz/1¼ cups) green beans, trimmed and cut into 2 cm (¾ inch) lengths, blanched

100 g (4 oz/⅔ cup) frozen peas, thawed

50 g (2 oz/⅓ cup) currants

1 small handful coriander (cilantro) leaves

2 tablespoons chopped toasted pistachio kernels

1 **Wash the rice** under cold water until it runs clear. Put the rice, saffron, cinnamon, cardamom pods, potato cubes and salt in a large saucepan. Fill with cold water to 2 cm (¾ inch) above the rice and bring to a simmer over low heat. When the rice starts to pocket (after about 5 minutes), cover and cook for 10 minutes, or until the rice is tender. Fluff the rice with a fork and turn out onto a flat tray to cool slightly. Discard the cinnamon stick and cardamom pods.

2 **Heat a wok** over high heat, add about 2 tablespoons of the oil and swirl to coat. Add the eggplant and stir-fry for about 4 minutes, or until softened and golden. Remove from wok.

3 **Heat the remaining oil** in the wok, add the onion and cook for 1 minute, or until softened. Add the garlic, ginger, chilli, spices and beans and cook for 1 minute.

4 **Stir in the rice mixture**, eggplant, peas, currants and coriander leaves and gently toss until combined. Serve sprinkled with the pistachios.

PAELLA

SERVES 4

500 g (1 lb 2 oz) black mussels
3 tablespoons olive oil
600 g (1 lb 5 oz) chicken drumettes or boneless, skinless chicken thighs halved
1 onion, chopped
2 large garlic cloves, chopped
3 vine-ripened tomatoes, peeled, seeded and finely chopped
1 small red capsicum (pepper), diced
1 small green capsicum (pepper), diced
¼ teaspoon chilli flakes
1 teaspoon paprika
¼ teaspoon saffron threads soaked in 3 tablespoons of warm water
290 g (11 oz/1⅓ cups) short-grain rice
1 litre (35 fl oz/4 cups) vegetable stock
12 raw prawns (shrimp), peeled, deveined, tails intact
155 g (6 oz/1 cup) peas
3 tablespoons dry sherry
4 tablespoons parsley, chopped
1 lemon, cut into wedges

1   **Scrub the mussels** and remove the beards. Discard any open mussels that don't close when tapped.

2   **Heat 2 tablespoons oil** in a large frying pan, add the chicken and cook over medium heat for 5–7 minutes, or until browned. Remove from the pan and keep warm.

3   **Add the remaining oil** to the pan, then add the onion, garlic and tomato, and cook over low heat for 5 minutes, or until soft.

4   **Add the capsicum** and cook for 1 minute, then stir in the chilli flakes, paprika and saffron and its soaking liquid. Pour in the rice and return the chicken to the pan. Add the stock, bring to the boil, then reduce the heat and simmer for 10 minutes.

5   **Stir in the prawns,** peas, sherry and mussels. Cover for 2 minutes, or until the mussels open. Discard any that do not open. Stir for 2 minutes, or until the prawns are pink and cooked through. Stir in the parsley. Serve immediately with the lemon wedges.

YANGZHOU-STYLE FRIED RICE

SERVES 4

2 tablespoons dried shrimp

3 tablespoons vegetable oil

3 eggs, lightly beaten

250 g (9 oz) Chinese barbecue pork (char siu), finely diced

100 g (4 oz/½ cup) tinned straw mushrooms, drained, rinsed and finely diced

740 g (1 lb 10 oz/4 cups) cooked long-grain rice, cold

2½ tablespoons light soy sauce

3 spring onions (scallions), finely chopped

2 tablespoons finely snipped garlic chives

white pepper, to taste

sesame oil, to taste

1 Put the dried shrimp in a heatproof bowl and cover with boiling water. Leave to soak for 15 minutes, then drain and finely chop.

2 Heat a wok until hot, add 1 tablespoon of oil and swirl to coat. Add the egg and leave it until it just starts to set. When the egg is almost cooked, break it into small strips with the edge of a spatula, then remove from the wok.

3 Heat another tablespoon of oil in the wok, add barbecue pork and stir-fry over high heat for 1 minute, or until heated through. Add the straw mushrooms and soaked shrimp, and continue to stir-fry with the pork for an additional 1–2 minutes.

4 Add the remaining oil, then gradually add the cooked rice, tossing and stirring for 2 minutes, or until heated through. Reduce heat to medium, add the soy sauce, spring onion and garlic chives, then continue to stir-fry until all the ingredients are thoroughly combined and the soy sauce evenly coats the rice. Season to taste with white pepper and a drizzle of sesame oil, and serve, topped with the omelette strips.

SICHUAN RICE NOODLES

SERVES 4

6 dried shiitake mushrooms

1 tablespoon Chinese rice wine

3 tablespoons kecap manis

1 tablespoon peanut oil

6 spring onions (scallions), cut into 3 cm (1¼ inch) lengths

2 garlic cloves, crushed

1 teaspoon Chinese five-spice

2 tablespoons chopped coriander (cilantro) stems and roots

1 teaspoon sichuan pepper, pounded

1 large long red chilli, thinly sliced on the diagonal

375 g (13 oz) baby bok choy (pak choy), quartered lengthways

500 g (1 lb 2 oz) fresh rice noodles, 2 cm (¾ inch) wide

1 small handful coriander (cilantro) leaves

2 spring onions (scallions), extra, finely sliced on the diagonal

1 **Soak the mushrooms** in boiling water for 5 minutes to soften. Drain, reserving 3 tablespoons of the liquid. Discard the woody stems and finely slice the caps. Combine the reserved liquid, rice wine and kecap manis.

2 **Heat a wok** over high heat, add the oil and swirl to coat. Stir-fry the spring onion, garlic, five-spice, coriander stems, pepper and chilli for 1–2 minutes.

3 **Add the bok choy,** mushrooms and the mushroom sauce mixture and stir-fry for a further 2 minutes, or until the bok choy has wilted. Add the noodles and gently toss until well combined and coated in the sauce. Serve sprinkled with the coriander leaves and extra spring onion.

GINGER CHICKEN STIR-FRY WITH HOKKIEN NOODLES

SERVES 4

2½ tablespoons finely shredded fresh ginger

3 tablespoons mirin

2 tablespoons soy sauce

600 g (1 lb 5 oz) chicken tenderloins or boneless, skinless, chicken breasts, cut diagonally into thin strips

180 g (6 oz) fresh baby corn

350 g (12 oz) choy sum

150 g (6 oz) fresh oyster mushrooms

500 g (1 lb 2 oz) hokkien (egg) noodles

2 tablespoons oil

2 tablespoons oyster sauce

1 **Combine the ginger,** mirin and soy sauce in a non-metallic bowl. Add the chicken, coat well, then marinate.

2 **Cut the corn** in half lengthways; trim the ends off the choy sum and cut into 6 cm (2½ inch) lengths.

3 **Soak the noodles** in a large heatproof bowl in boiling water for 5 minutes. Drain; refresh under cold running water.

4 **Heat 1 tablespoon of the oil** in a wok until very hot. Remove the chicken from the marinade with a slotted spoon. Cook in two batches over very high heat for 2 minutes, or until brown and just cooked. Remove from the wok.

5 **Add the remaining oil** to the wok and stir-fry mushrooms and corn for 1–2 minutes, or until just softened. Add remaining marinade and bring to the boil.

6 **Add the chicken,** choy sum and noodles. Stir in the oyster sauce and cook, tossing well, for 1–2 minutes, or until the choy sum has wilted slightly and the noodles are warmed through.

RICE NOODLES WITH BEEF, BLACK BEANS AND CAPSICUMS

SERVES 4

300 g (11 oz) rump steak

1 garlic clove, crushed

3 tablespoons oyster sauce

2 teaspoons sugar

2 tablespoons soy sauce

5 tablespoons black bean sauce

2 teaspoons cornflour (cornstarch)

¾ teaspoon sesame oil

1.2 kg (2 lb 11 oz) fresh or 600 g (1 lb 5 oz) dried flat rice noodles

1½ tablespoons oil

2 red capsicums (peppers), sliced

1 green capsicum (pepper), sliced

1 handful coriander (cilantro) leaves

1 Cut the steak across the grain into thin slices. Combine the garlic, oyster sauce, sugar, soy sauce, black bean sauce, cornflour and sesame oil in a bowl. Add the steak, making sure the slices are all well coated.

2 If you are using dried rice noodles. soak them in boiling water for 10 minutes, or until opaque and soft. Drain well.

3 Heat the oil in a wok or frying pan and add the capsicum. Stir-fry for 1–2 minutes or until they start to soften, then add the meat mixture and cook for a minute.

4 Add the noodles and gently toss to combine. Cook until the meat is cooked through, then toss in the coriander leaves and stir. Serve immediately.

SPICY CELLOPHANE NOODLES WITH MINCED PORK

SERVES 4

200 g (7 oz) minced (ground) pork

1 teaspoon cornflour (cornstarch)

1½ tablespoons light soy sauce

2 tablespoons Chinese rice wine

1 teaspoon sesame oil

150 g (6 oz) cellophane noodles (mung bean vermicelli)

2 tablespoons oil

4 spring onions (scallions), finely chopped

1 garlic clove, crushed

1 tablespoon finely chopped ginger

2 teaspoons chilli bean sauce

185 ml (6 fl oz/¾ cup) chicken stock

½ teaspoon sugar

2 spring onions (scallions), green part only, extra, thinly sliced on the diagonal

1 **Combine the pork,** cornflour, 1 tablespoon of the soy sauce, 1 tablespoon of the rice wine and ½ teaspoon of the sesame oil in a bowl. Cover with plastic wrap and marinate for about 10–15 minutes.

2 **Meanwhile,** place the noodles in a heatproof bowl. Cover with boiling water and soak for 3–4 minutes, or until softened. Drain well.

3 **Heat the oil** in a wok over high heat. Cook the spring onion, garlic, ginger and chilli bean sauce for 10 seconds, then add the mince mixture and cook for about 2 minutes, stirring to break up any lumps. Stir in the stock, sugar, ½ teaspoon salt, and the remaining soy sauce, rice wine and sesame oil.

4 **Add the noodles** to the wok and toss to combine. Bring to the boil, then reduce the heat to low and simmer, stirring occasionally, for 7–8 minutes, or until the liquid is almost completely absorbed. Garnish with the extra spring onion and serve.

INDONESIAN-STYLE FRIED NOODLES

SERVES 4

400 g (14 oz) fresh flat egg noodles
(5 mm/¼ inch wide)

2 tablespoons peanut oil

4 red Asian shallots, thinly sliced

2 garlic cloves, chopped

1 small red chilli, finely diced

200 g (7 oz) pork fillet, thinly sliced
across the grain

200 g (7 oz) boneless, skinless chicken
breasts, thinly sliced

200 g (7 oz) small raw prawns (shrimp),
peeled and deveined, with tails intact

2 Chinese cabbage leaves, shredded

2 carrots, cut in half lengthways and
thinly sliced

100 g (4 oz) snake (yard long) beans,
cut into 3 cm (1¼ inch) lengths

3 tablespoons kecap manis

1 tablespoon light soy sauce

2 tomatoes, peeled, seeded and
chopped

4 spring onions (scallions), sliced on the
diagonal

1 tablespoon crisp fried onion flakes

flat-leaf (Italian) parsley, to garnish

1 **Cook the noodles** in a large saucepan of boiling water for 1 minute, or until tender. Drain and rinse them under cold water.

2 **Heat a wok** over high heat, add the oil and swirl to coat. Stir-fry the Asian shallots for 30 seconds. Add the garlic, chilli and pork and stir-fry for 2 minutes. Add the chicken and cook a further 2 minutes, or until the meat is golden and tender.

3 **Add the prawns** and stir-fry for a further 2 minutes, or until pink and just cooked. Stir in the cabbage, carrot and beans and cook for 3 minutes.

4 **Add the noodles** and gently stir-fry for about 4 minutes, or until heated through — taking care not to break up the noodles. Stir in the kecap manis, soy sauce, chopped tomato and spring onion and stir-fry for 1–2 minutes.

5 **Season with salt** and freshly ground black pepper. Garnish with the fried onion flakes and parsley.

Note: This dish, called bahmi goreng in Indonesian, is traditionally eaten with chopped roasted peanuts and sambal oelek on the side. It is also delicious with satay sauce.

SINGAPORE NOODLES

SERVES 4

2 tablespoons dried shrimp

300 g (11 oz) rice vermicelli

100 g (4 oz) Chinese barbecue pork
(char siu)

100 g (4 oz) bean sprouts, trimmed

4 tablespoons oil

2 eggs, beaten

1 onion, thinly sliced

1 teaspoon salt

1 tablespoon Chinese curry powder

2 tablespoons light soy sauce

2 spring onions (scallions) shredded

2 red chillies, shredded

1   Soak the dried shrimp in boiling water for 1 hour, then drain. Soak the noodles in hot water for 10 minutes, then drain. Thinly slice the pork. Wash the bean sprouts and drain thoroughly.

2   Heat 1 tablespoon of the oil in a wok over high heat until very hot. Pour in the egg and make an omelette. Remove from the wok and cut into pieces.

3   Reheat the wok over high heat, add the remaining oil and heat until very hot. Stir-fry the onion and bean sprouts with the pork and shrimp for 1 minute.

4   Add the noodles, salt, curry powder and soy sauce, blend well and stir for 1 minute. Add the omelette, spring onion and chilli and toss to combine.

SHANGHAI PORK NOODLES

SERVES 4

½ teaspoon sesame oil

3 tablespoons soy sauce

2 tablespoons oyster sauce

250 g (9 oz) pork loin fillet, cut into very thin strips

2 tablespoons dried shrimp

8 dried shiitake mushrooms

1 teaspoon sugar

250 ml (9 fl oz/1 cup) chicken stock

300 g (11 oz) fresh Shanghai noodles

2 tablespoons peanut oil

1 garlic clove, thinly sliced

2 teaspoons grated fresh ginger

1 celery stalk, cut into matchsticks

1 leek, white part only, cut into matchsticks

150 g (6 oz) Chinese cabbage (wong bok), shredded

50 g (2 oz) tinned bamboo shoots, cut into matchsticks

8 spring onions (scallions), thinly sliced

1 Combine the sesame oil and 1 tablespoon each of the soy sauce and oyster sauce. Add the pork strips. Marinate for 30 minutes.

2 Meanwhile, put the dried shrimp in a bowl, cover with boiling water and soak for about 20 minutes. Drain and then finely chop.

3 Meanwhile, put the shiitake mushrooms in a heatproof bowl, cover with boiling water and soak for 20 minutes. Drain, squeeze dry, discard the stems and thinly slice the caps.

4 To make the stir-fry sauce, combine the sugar, stock, remaining soy and oyster sauces and 1 teaspoon salt in a bowl. Set aside.

5 Cook the noodles in a saucepan of boiling water for about 5 minutes, or until tender. Drain and refresh under cold water. Toss with 1 teaspoon of the peanut oil.

6 Heat 1 tablespoon of the peanut oil in a wok over high heat. Add the pork and stir-fry for 1–2 minutes, or until cooked. Remove to a plate.

7 Heat the remaining peanut oil, add the garlic, ginger, celery, leek and cabbage and stir-fry for 1 minute, or until softened. Add the bamboo shoots, spring onion, shrimp and mushrooms and stir-fry for 1 minute.

8 Add the noodles and the stir-fry sauce and toss together for 3–5 minutes.

9 Return the pork to the wok, with any juices, and toss for 1–2 minutes.

UDON NOODLE SOUP

SERVES 4

400 g (14 oz) dried udon noodles

1 litre (35 fl oz/4 cups) water

3 teaspoons dashi granules

2 leeks, white part only, finely sliced

200 g (7 oz) pork loin, cut into thin strips

125 ml (4 fl oz/½ cup) Japanese
   soy sauce

2 tablespoons mirin

4 spring onions (scallions), finely
   chopped

shichimi togarashi (see Note), to serve

1 Cook the noodles in a large saucepan of rapidly boiling water for 5 minutes, or until tender. Drain and cover to keep warm.

2 Combine the water and dashi in a large saucepan and bring to the boil. Add the leek, reduce the heat and simmer for 5 minutes. Add the pork, soy sauce, mirin and spring onion and simmer for 2 minutes, or until the pork is cooked. Divide the noodles among four serving bowls and ladle the soup over the top. Garnish with the spring onion and sprinkle the shichimi togarashi over the top.

Note: Shichimi togarashi is a Japanese spice mix. It is available in Asian grocery stores, as are dashi granules.

STIR-FRIED LAMB WITH MINT, CHILLI AND NOODLES

SERVES 4–6

400 g (14 oz) Shanghai noodles

1 teaspoon sesame oil

2 tablespoons peanut oil

220 g (8 oz) lamb fillet, cut into thin strips

2 garlic cloves, crushed

2 fresh red chillies, seeded and finely sliced

1 tablespoon oyster sauce

2 teaspoons palm sugar (jaggery) or soft brown sugar

2 tablespoons fish sauce

2 tablespoons lime juice

10 g (¼ oz) mint, chopped

lime wedges, to garnish

1 Cook the noodles in a large saucepan of boiling water for 4–5 minutes. Drain, then rinse in cold water. Add the sesame oil and toss through.

2 Heat the peanut oil in a wok over high heat. Add the lamb and cook in batches for 1–2 minutes, or until just browned. Return all the meat to the wok and add the garlic and chilli. Cook for 30 seconds.

3 Add the oyster sauce, palm sugar, fish sauce, lime juice and noodles. Cook for a further 2–3 minutes, or until the noodles are warm. Stir in the mint and serve immediately with the lime wedges.

CHILLI AND TOFU NOODLES

SERVES 6

3 tablespoons peanut oil

1 teaspoon bottled crushed chilli

2 teaspoons grated fresh ginger

2 garlic cloves, crushed

250 g (9 oz) hard tofu, cut into small cubes

8 spring onions (scallions), sliced on the diagonal

150 g (6 oz) fresh baby corn, halved lengthways

150 g (6 oz) snowpeas (mangetout), topped and tailed

500 g (1 lb 2 oz) hokkien (egg) noodles

40 g (1½ oz/¼ cup) cashew nuts

2 tablespoons soy sauce

125 ml (4 fl oz/½ cup) vegetable stock

1 handful coriander (cilantro) leaves

1 **Heat the oil** in a wok over medium heat and swirl to coat. Add chilli, ginger and garlic and stir-fry for about 3 minutes, or until aromatic. Add the tofu cubes, spring onion and baby corn and stir-fry for 2–3 minutes.

2 **Add the snowpeas,** noodles and cashews and cook, stirring, for 3–5 minutes, or until the vegetables are almost tender. Stir in the soy sauce and stock, then bring to the boil and simmer for 2 minutes, or until slightly reduced. Stir in the coriander and serve immediately.

SPICY CHILLI PRAWNS WITH HOKKIEN NOODLES

400 g (14 oz) hokkien (egg) noodles

1 tablespoon peanut oil

1 tablespoon red curry paste

2 garlic cloves, crushed

1 lemongrass stem (white part only), finely chopped

2 tablespoons finely sliced coriander (cilantro) root

125 ml (4 fl oz/½ cup) lime juice

60 g (2 oz/⅓ cup) grated palm sugar (jaggery) or soft brown sugar

2 tablespoons tomato sauce (ketchup)

2½ tablespoons fish sauce

185 ml (6 fl oz/¾ cup) chicken stock

16 prawns (shrimp), peeled and deveined

350 g (12 oz) choy sum, cut into 2 cm (¾ inch) lengths

100 g (4 oz) snake (yard long) beans, cut into 1.5 cm (⅝ inch) lengths

4 spring onions (scallions), finely chopped

115 g (4 oz/¾ cup) roasted cashew nuts, roughly chopped

3 tablespoons coriander (cilantro) leaves

Thai basil, to garnish

lime wedges, to serve (optional)

1 **Place the noodles** in a heatproof bowl, cover with boiling water and soak for 1 minute, or until tender. Drain, rinse under cold water and drain again.

2 **Heat a wok** over high heat, add the oil and swirl to coat. Add the curry paste and fry for 5 seconds, then add the garlic, lemongrass and coriander root and stir-fry for 30 seconds, or until well combined.

3 **Whisk the lime juice,** palm sugar, tomato sauce, fish sauce and stock together, then add to the wok. Cook over high heat for 2 minutes, or until slightly reduced.

4 **Add the prawns** and cook for 2–3 minutes, or until almost cooked. Add the noodles and stir-fry for 2 minutes. Add the choy sum and beans and continue to stir-fry for 2 minutes, or until the leaves have wilted and the beans are tender but not soft.

5 **Stir in the spring onion,** cashews and coriander leaves until combined. Garnish with the basil and serve with lime wedges.

IDIYAPPAM

SERVES 4

225 g (8 oz) rice sticks or vermicelli

4 tablespoons oil

50 g (2 oz/⅓ cup) cashew nuts

1 small onion, chopped

3 eggs

150 g (6 oz/1 cup) fresh or frozen peas

10 curry leaves

2 carrots, grated

2 leeks, finely shredded

1 red capsicum (pepper), diced

2 tablespoons tomato sauce (ketchup)

1 tablespoon soy sauce

1 teaspoon salt

1 Soak the rice sticks in cold water for 30 minutes, then drain and put them in a saucepan of boiling water. Remove from the heat and leave in the pan for 3 minutes. Drain and refresh in cold water.

2 Heat 1 tablespoon of the oil in a frying pan and fry the cashews until golden. Remove. Add the onion to the pan, fry until dark golden, then drain.

3 Cook the eggs in boiling water for about 10 minutes to hard-boil, then cool in cold water. When cold, peel and cut into wedges. Cook the peas in boiling water until tender.

4 Heat the oil in a pan and fry the curry leaves. Add the carrot, leek and capsicum and stir for 1 minute. Add the tomato sauce, soy sauce, salt and rice sticks. Serve with the peas, cashews, fried onion and egg.

BUDDHIST VEGETARIAN NOODLES

SERVES 4

15 g (½ oz) dried Chinese mushrooms

400 g (14 oz) fresh flat egg noodles

2–3 tablespoons peanut oil

1 small carrot, cut into thin matchsticks

150 g (6 oz) baby corn, cut into quarters lengthways

230 g (8 oz) tinned sliced bamboo shoots, drained

150 g (6 oz) snowpeas (mangetout), cut into thin strips

½ small red capsicum (pepper), cut into thin strips

1 small green capsicum (pepper), cut into thin strips

90 g (3¼ oz) bean sprouts, trimmed

40 g (1½ oz) Chinese cabbage (wong bok), finely shredded

2 cm (¾ inch) piece ginger, cut into very fine strips

1 tablespoon mushroom soy sauce

1 tablespoon light soy sauce

1 tablespoon Chinese rice wine

2 tablespoons vegetarian oyster sauce

1 teaspoon sesame oil

ground white pepper, to taste

2 tablespoons coriander (cilantro) leaves

1 Place the Chinese mushrooms in a heatproof bowl, cover with boiling water and soak for 20 minutes. Drain. Discard the woody stems and thinly slice the caps.

2 Meanwhile, cook the noodles in a large saucepan of boiling water for 1 minute. Drain. Rinse under cold water and drain again.

3 Heat 1 tablespoon of oil in a wok over high heat. Stir-fry carrot and corn for 1–2 minutes, then add the bamboo shoots and stir-fry for 1–2 minutes, or until just cooked. Remove and set aside.

4 Add the snowpeas and red and green capsicum to the wok. Stir-fry for 2 minutes, or until just cooked. Add to the carrot and corn mixture.

5 Add the bean sprouts, cabbage and mushrooms to the wok and stir-fry for 30 seconds, or until wilted. Add the ginger and stir-fry for another 1–2 minutes. Remove and add to the other vegetables.

6 Heat the remaining oil in the wok, and stir-fry the noodles for 1–2 minutes, or until heated through. Stir in the mushroom soy sauce, light soy sauce, rice wine and oyster sauce. Return all the vegetables to the wok and stir for about 2 minutes. Drizzle with the sesame oil, season and garnish with the coriander leaves.

LEMONGRASS BEEF NOODLES

SERVES 4

DRESSING

125 ml (4 fl oz/½ cup) lime juice

4 tablespoons fish sauce

1 tablespoon caster (superfine) sugar

4 tablespoons warm water

1–2 small red chillies, finely chopped

1 small garlic clove, finely chopped

MARINADE

3 lemongrass stems, white part chopped

2 garlic cloves, crushed

1 tablespoon fish sauce

1 tablespoon light soy sauce

2 teaspoons caster (superfine) sugar

1 teaspoon vegetable oil

500 g (1 lb 2 oz) beef fillet, thinly sliced

240 g (8 oz) dried rice vermicelli

1–2 tablespoons peanut oil

1 small Lebanese (short) cucumber

1 small carrot

150 g (6 oz) bean sprouts, tails trimmed

1 handful coriander (cilantro) leaves

1 handful Vietnamese mint leaves,
    plus extra for garnish

70 g (2 oz) ground unsalted toasted
    peanuts

1 **To make the dressing,** combine all the ingredients, stirring until the sugar has completely dissolved. Cover and set aside.

2 **To make the marinade,** put all the ingredients in a food processor and pulse to form a smooth paste. Put the beef slices in a bowl, cover with the marinade and stir to coat. Cover with plastic wrap and refrigerate for at least 2 hours.

3 **Soak the rice vermicelli** in boiling water for 5 minutes. Drain, rinse and drain again.

4 **Heat a wok** to high, add 1 tablespoon of the oil and swirl to coat. Add the beef in batches and sear for 2–3 minutes.

5 **Place vermicelli in a bowl.** Slice the cucumber and carrot into thin strips and add to vermicelli with the bean sprouts, coriander and mint leaves. Add the dressing and toss well to combine. Top with beef, extra mint leaves and peanuts.

HOKKIEN MEE

SERVES 4

400 g (14 oz) hokkien (egg) noodles

350 g (12 oz) prawns (shrimp)

2 tablespoons peanut oil

3 garlic cloves, finely chopped

200 g (7 oz) Chinese barbecued pork (char siu), thinly sliced

400 g (14 oz) baby bok choy (pak choy), trimmed and leaves separated

250 ml (9 fl oz/1 cup) hot chicken stock

2 tablespoons dark soy sauce

1 tablespoon oyster sauce

½ teaspoon sugar

90 g (3 oz) bean sprouts, trimmed

1   Place the noodles in a heatproof bowl, cover with boiling water and soak for 1 minute, or until tender. Drain and rinse.

2   To peel the prawns, remove the tails, and gently pull out the vein from the backs, starting at the head end. Remove the tails.

3   Heat 1 tablespoon of the peanut oil in a wok over high heat. Add the prawns and garlic and cook for 1–2 minutes, or until just cooked through. Remove from the wok.

4   Heat the remaining oil in the wok over high heat, add the noodles, pork and bok choy and cook for 3–4 minutes.

5   Add the chicken stock, soy and oyster sauces, and the sugar. Return the prawn and garlic mixture to the wok with the bean sprouts and stir for 1–2 minutes, or until heated through.

THAI-STYLE CHICKEN NOODLE SOUP

SERVES 4

425 g (15 oz) tinned corn kernels, undrained

2 chicken stock (bouillon) cubes, crumbled

8 spring onions (scallions), sliced

1 tablespoon finely chopped fresh ginger

500 g (1 lb 2 oz) skinless chicken breast, trimmed and thinly sliced

1 tablespoon sweet chilli sauce

1 tablespoon fish sauce

200 g (7 oz) fresh thin rice noodles

2 large handfuls coriander (cilantro) leaves, chopped

2 teaspoons grated lime zest

2 tablespoons lime juice

1 Bring 1 litre (35 fl oz/4 cups) water to the boil in a large saucepan over high heat. Add the corn kernels and their juice, the stock cubes, spring onion and ginger, then reduce the heat and simmer for 1 minute.

2 Add the chicken, sweet chilli sauce and fish sauce and simmer for 3 minutes, or until the chicken is cooked through.

3 Put noodles in a large heatproof bowl, cover with boiling water and soak for 5 minutes, or until softened. Separate gently and drain.

4 Add the noodles, coriander, lime zest and lime juice to the soup and serve immediately.

LAKSA

200 g (7 oz) dried rice vermicelli

2 tablespoons peanut oil

2–3 tablespoons laksa paste

1 litre (35 fl oz/4 cups) vegetable stock

750 ml (26 fl oz/3 cups) coconut milk

250 g (9 oz) snowpeas (mangetout), halved diagonally

5 spring onions (scallions), cut into 3 cm (1¼ inch) lengths

2 tablespoons lime juice

125 g (5 oz) bean sprouts, trimmed

200 g (7 oz) fried tofu puffs, halved

3 tablespoons roughly chopped Vietnamese mint

4 tablespoons coriander (cilantro) leaves

1 Put the vermicelli in a large bowl, cover with boiling water and soak for 5 minutes.

2 Heat the oil in a large saucepan, add the laksa paste and cook, stirring, over medium heat for 1 minute, or until fragrant.

3 Add the stock, coconut milk, snowpeas and spring onion and simmer for 5 minutes. Pour in lime juice; season to taste.

4 Drain the vermicelli and add the bean sprouts and fried tofu puffs. Ladle the hot soup over the vermicelli and serve immediately, sprinkled with the mint and coriander.

GREEN CURRY CHICKEN NOODLE STIR-FRY

SERVES 4

400 g (14 oz) hokkien (egg) noodles

1 tablespoon peanut oil

1 onion, cut into thin wedges

1½ tablespoons good-quality green
    curry paste

150 g (6 oz) baby corn, cut in half on
    the diagonal

125 g (5 oz) snake (yard long) beans, cut
    into 4 cm (1½ inch) lengths

250 ml (9 fl oz/1 cup) coconut milk

125 ml (4 fl oz/½ cup) chicken stock

500 g (1 lb 2 oz) boneless, skinless
    chicken breast, cut into 1 cm (½ inch)
    strips

2 teaspoons grated palm (jaggery) sugar
    or soft brown sugar

1 tablespoon fish sauce

2 teaspoons lime juice

3 tablespoons chopped coriander
    (cilantro) leaves

coriander (cilantro) leaves, extra,
    to garnish

1   Place the noodles in a heatproof bowl, cover with boiling water and soak for 1 minute, or until tender and separated. Drain thoroughly.

2   Heat a wok over high heat, add the oil and swirl to coat. Stir-fry the onion for 1–2 minutes, or until softened. Add the curry paste and cook for 1 minute, or until fragrant.

3   Add the baby corn, snake beans, coconut milk and stock to the wok and simmer for 3–4 minutes. Add the chicken, and continue to cook for another 3–4 minutes, or until the chicken is cooked.

4   Stir the palm sugar, fish sauce and lime juice into the wok. Add the noodles and chopped coriander and toss until well combined and the noodles are warmed through. Serve immediately, garnished with the extra coriander leaves.

CURRY MEE NOODLES

SERVES 4

2 large dried red chillies

1 teaspoon shrimp paste

400 g (14 oz) hokkien (egg) noodles

1 onion, chopped

4 garlic cloves, chopped

4 lemongrass stems, white part only, thinly sliced

1 teaspoon grated fresh ginger

500 ml (17 fl oz/2 cups) coconut cream

25 g (1 oz/¼ cup) Malaysian curry powder

400 g (14 oz) boneless, skinless chicken thighs, thinly sliced

120 g (4 oz) green beans, trimmed and cut into 5 cm (2 inch) lengths

750 ml (26 fl oz/3 cups) chicken stock

10 fried tofu puffs, halved diagonally

2 tablespoons fish sauce

2 teaspoons sugar

180 g (6 oz) bean sprouts

2 hard-boiled eggs, quartered

2 tablespoons crisp fried shallots

lime wedges, to serve

1 **Soak the chillies** in boiling water for 20 minutes. Drain, then chop. Wrap the shrimp paste in foil and put under a hot grill (broiler) for 1–2 minutes. Unwrap.

2 **Put the noodles** in a bowl, cover with boiling water and soak for 1 minute to separate. Rinse under cold water; drain.

3 **Put the onion,** garlic, lemongrass, ginger, chilli and shrimp paste in a food processor or blender and process to a rough paste, adding a little water if necessary.

4 **Put 250 ml** (9fl oz/1 cup) of the coconut cream in a wok and bring to the boil, then simmer for 10 minutes, or until the oil starts to separate from the cream. Stir in the paste and curry powder and cook for 5 minutes. Add the chicken and beans and cook for 3–4 minutes, or until the chicken is almost cooked. Add the stock, tofu puffs, fish sauce, sugar and the remaining coconut cream. Simmer, covered, over low heat for 10 minutes, or until chicken is cooked.

5 **Divide the noodles** and bean sprouts among four bowls, then ladle the curry over the top. Garnish with the egg quarters and crisp fried shallots. Serve with lime wedges.

DAN DAN NOODLES

SERVES 4

1 tablespoon Chinese rice wine

½ teaspoon sesame oil

1 teaspoon chilli oil

3 tablespoons light soy sauce

500 g (1 lb 2 oz) minced (ground) chicken

1 tablespoon peanut oil

2 garlic cloves, finely chopped

1 teaspoon finely chopped ginger

2 teaspoons chilli bean paste

1 tablespoon Chinese sesame paste

185 ml (6 fl oz/¾ cup) chicken stock

1 tablespoon oyster sauce

375 g (13 oz) fresh flat egg noodles

3 spring onions (scallions), thinly sliced on the diagonal

1 **Combine rice wine,** sesame oil, chilli oil and 2 tablespoons soy sauce in a bowl. Add minced chicken and mix well. Cover with plastic wrap and marinate for 20 minutes.

2 **Heat a wok** over high heat, add the peanut oil and swirl to coat. Add the garlic, ginger and chilli bean paste and stir-fry for 1 minute, or until fragrant.

3 **Add chicken mixture** and cook for 2–3 minutes, or until browned, stirring to break up any lumps. Stir in sesame paste, chicken stock, oyster sauce and remaining soy sauce, then reduce the heat to medium–low and simmer for 20 minutes.

4 **Meanwhile,** cook noodles in a saucepan of boiling water for 1 minute, or until tender. Drain, rinse, then drain again.

5 **Stir the spring onion** through the chicken mixture, then spoon over the noodles.

PHAD THAI

SERVES 4–6

250 g (9 oz) dried rice stick noodles

1 tablespoon tamarind purée

1 small red chilli, chopped

2 garlic cloves, chopped

2 spring onions (scallions), sliced

1½ tablespoons sugar

2 tablespoons fish sauce

2 tablespoons lime juice

2 tablespoons oil

2 eggs, beaten

8 large raw prawns (shrimp)

150 g (6 oz) pork fillet, thinly sliced

100 g (4 oz) fried tofu puffs, cut into thin strips

90 g (3 oz) bean sprouts

40 g (1½ oz/¼ cup) chopped roasted peanuts

3 tablespoons coriander (cilantro) leaves

1 lime, cut into wedges

1 **Put the noodles** in a heatproof bowl, cover with warm water and soak for 15–20 minutes, or until soft and pliable. Drain well.

2 **Combine the tamarind purée** with 1 tablespoon water. Put chilli, garlic and spring onion in a spice grinder or mortar and pestle and grind to a smooth paste. Transfer to a bowl.

3 **Stir in tamarind mixture** along with the sugar, fish sauce and lime juice, stirring until combined.

4 **Heat a wok** until hot. Add 1 tablespoon of the oil and swirl to coat the base and side. Add the egg, swirl to coat and cook for about 1–2 minutes, or until set. Remove, roll up and cut into thin slices.

5 **Peel the prawns** and gently pull out the dark vein from each prawn back, starting from the head end.

6 **Heat the remaining oil** in the wok, stir in the chilli mixture and stir-fry for 30 seconds. Add pork and stir-fry for 2 minutes, or until tender. Add prawns and stir-fry for a further minute, or until pink and curled.

7 **Stir in the noodles,** egg, tofu and bean sprouts and gently toss everything together until heated through. Serve at once topped with the peanuts, coriander and lime wedges.

MEAT & CHICKEN

STEAK WITH GREEN PEPPERCORN SAUCE

SERVES 4

4 x 200 g (7 oz) fillet steaks

30 g (1 oz) butter

2 teaspoons oil

250 ml (9 fl oz/1 cup) beef stock

185 ml (6 fl oz/¾ cup) thick (double/ heavy) cream

2 teaspoons cornflour (cornstarch)

2 tablespoons green peppercorns in brine, rinsed and drained

2 tablespoons brandy

potato chips, to serve (optional)

rosemary, to garnish

1 **Bash the steaks** with a meat mallet to 1.5 cm (⅝ inch) thick. Next, nick the edges of the steaks to prevent them from curling when they are cooking.

2 **Heat the butter** and oil in a large heavy-based frying pan over high heat. Fry the steaks for 2–4 minutes on each side, depending on how you like your steak. Transfer to a serving plate and cover with foil.

3 **Add the stock** to the pan juices and stir over low heat until boiling. Combine the cream and cornflour, then pour the mixture into the pan and stir constantly until the sauce becomes smooth and thick — a few minutes will do. Add the peppercorns and brandy and boil for 1 more minute before taking the pan off the heat. Spoon the sauce over the steaks. Serve with potato chips and garnish with rosemary.

PORK CHOPS WITH RED ONION AND APPLE

SERVES 4

125 g (4 oz) butter

2 small red onions, sliced

2 granny smith apples, peeled, cored, then cut into quarters and sliced

¼ teaspoon ground cloves

115 g (7 oz/⅓ cup) honey

4 pork loin chops (about 250 g/8 oz each)

2 teaspoons oil

½ teaspoon caraway seeds

725 g (1 lb 10 oz) green cabbage, thinly shredded

1 **To make the chutney,** melt 50 g (2 oz) of the butter in a saucepan, then add the onion, apple, cloves and honey. Simmer, covered, for 10 minutes over low heat. Increase the heat to medium, cover and cook for another 20 minutes, or until the liquid is reduced to a thick chutney. Allow to cool.

2 **Meanwhile, season chops** well on both sides with salt and freshly ground black pepper. Heat the oil and 50 g (2 oz) of the butter in a large frying pan and sauté the chops over medium–high heat for 6–8 minutes on each side, or until browned and cooked through. Remove pan from the heat, leaving the chops to rest for 2 minutes.

3 **While the chops** are cooking, melt the remaining butter in a large saucepan, add the caraway seeds and cabbage and cook, covered, over medium–low heat, tossing a few times with tongs, for 12 minutes, or until tender.

4 **Place a pork chop** on each plate and serve the cabbage on the side. Top with a spoonful of chutney.

PAN-FRIED LAMB FILLETS WITH RED WINE

SERVES 4

600 g (1 lb 5 oz) small new potatoes

160 g (5¾ oz) snowpeas (mangetout), trimmed

2 tablespoons olive oil

4 lamb backstraps or eye of loin fillets (about 200 g/7 oz each), trimmed

170 ml (6 fl oz/⅔ cup) red wine

1 tablespoon redcurrant jelly

2 teaspoons chopped thyme

30 g (1 oz) butter, chilled and cut into cubes

1 Cook the potatoes in a large saucepan of lightly salted boiling water for about 15–20 minutes, or until tender. Add the snowpeas and cook for another minute. Drain the vegetables, return to the pan and toss gently with 1 tablespoon of the oil.

2 Meanwhile, heat the remaining oil in a large frying pan and cook the lamb fillets over medium–high heat for about 4–5 minutes each side, or until cooked, but still pink inside. Remove from the pan, cover and keep warm.

3 Add the wine, redcurrant jelly and thyme to the pan and bring to the boil. Boil rapidly for 5 minutes, or until reduced and syrupy. Stir in the butter.

4 To serve, slice the lamb on the diagonal, divide among four plates and spoon some sauce on top. Serve immediately with the vegetables.

RED WINE STEAKS WITH BARBECUED VEGETABLES

SERVES 4

12 small new potatoes

3 tablespoons olive oil

1 tablespoon finely chopped fresh rosemary

6 garlic cloves, sliced

sea salt flakes, to season

4 large, thick field mushrooms

12 asparagus spears

250 ml (9 fl oz/1 cup) red wine

4 scotch fillet steaks (about 260 g/ 9 oz each)

1 **Heat a barbecue plate** or chargrill pan to hot. Toss the potatoes with 1 tablespoon of the oil, half the rosemary and half the garlic and season with the sea salt flakes. Divide the potatoes among four large sheets of foil and wrap into neat packages, sealing firmly around the edges. Cook on the barbecue, turning frequently for 30 minutes, or until tender.

2 **Meanwhile,** brush the mushrooms and asparagus with a little of the remaining oil and set aside.

3 **Combine the red wine** with the remaining oil, rosemary and garlic in a non-metallic dish. Season with lots of freshly ground black pepper. Add the steaks and coat in the marinade. Allow to marinate for 25 minutes, then drain.

4 **Cook steaks** and mushrooms on the barbecue for 4 minutes each side, or until cooked to your liking (this will depend on the thickness of the steak). Transfer the steaks and mushrooms to a plate, cover lightly and allow to rest. Add asparagus to the barbecue, turning regularly for 2 minutes, or until tender. Pierce the potatoes with a skewer to check for doneness. Season with salt and pepper. Serve the steaks with the vegetables.

GRILLED CHICKEN WITH CAPSICUM COUSCOUS

SERVES 4

200 g (7 oz/1 cup) instant couscous

1 tablespoon olive oil

1 onion, finely chopped

2 zucchini (courgettes), sliced

½ red or yellow chargrilled capsicum (pepper), chopped

12 semi-dried (sun-blushed) tomatoes, chopped

½ tablespoon grated orange zest

250 ml (9 fl oz/1 cup) orange juice

a large handful chopped mint

8 boneless, skinless chicken thighs or 4 chicken breasts, skin on

40 g (1½ oz) butter, softened

1 **Heat the grill** (broiler). Bring 500 ml (17 fl oz/2 cups) water to the boil in a saucepan, throw in the couscous, then take the pan off the heat and leave it to stand for 10 minutes.

2 **Heat the oil** in a frying pan. Fry the onion and zucchini until lightly browned. Add the capsicum and semi-dried tomatoes, then stir in the couscous. Stir in the orange zest, one-third of the orange juice and the mint.

3 **Put the chicken** in a large shallow baking dish in a single layer and dot it with the butter. Sprinkle with the remaining orange juice and season well with salt and pepper. Grill the chicken for 8 to 10 minutes, turning it over halfway through.

4 **Serve the chicken** on the couscous with any juices poured over it.

PARMESAN AND ROSEMARY VEAL CHOPS

SERVES 4

4 veal chops

150 g (6 oz) fresh white breadcrumbs

75 g (3 oz/¾ cup) freshly grated
  parmesan cheese

1 tablespoon rosemary, finely chopped

2 eggs, lightly beaten, seasoned

3 tablespoons olive oil

60 g (2 oz) butter

4 garlic cloves

1 Trim chops of excess fat and sinew and flatten to 1 cm (½ inch) thickness. Pat meat dry with paper towels. Combine the breadcrumbs, parmesan and rosemary in a shallow bowl.

2 Dip each chop in the beaten egg, draining off the excess. Press both sides of the chops firmly in the crumbs.

3 Heat oil and butter in a heavy-based frying pan over low heat, add the garlic and cook until golden. Discard the garlic.

4 Increase the heat to medium, add the chops to the pan and cook for 4–5 minutes on each side, depending on the thickness of the chops, until golden and crisp.

PORK CHOPS IN MARSALA

SERVES 4

4 pork loin chops

2 tablespoons olive oil

125 ml (4 fl oz/½ cup) Marsala (see Note)

2 teaspoons grated orange zest

3 tablespoons orange juice

3 tablespoons chopped flat-leaf (Italian) parsley

1 **Pat dry the chops** and season well. Heat the olive oil in a heavy-based frying pan over medium heat and cook the chops on both sides for 5 minutes each side, or until brown and cooked.

2 **Add the Marsala**, orange zest and juice and cook for 4–5 minutes, or until the sauce has reduced and thickened. Add the parsley and serve immediately.

Note: Marsala is a fortified wine from Sicily, made by mixing grape juice with white wine, which is then left to mature in casks. Marsala has a sweet, smoky flavour that ranges from dry to sweet. Some may be flavoured with almond, cream or egg. Dry Marsala is best for use in cooking and appears in many sauces for various Italian dishes such as saltimbocca and chicken cacciatora. You can find it in most large supermarkets or delicatessens.

LAMB CUTLETS WITH MINT GREMOLATA

SERVES 4

4 tablespoons mint leaves

1 tablespoon flat-leaf (Italian) parsley

2 garlic cloves

1½ tablespoons lemon zest (white pith removed), cut into thin strips

2 tablespoons extra virgin olive oil

8 French-trimmed lamb cutlets

2 carrots

2 zucchini (courgettes)

1 tablespoon lemon juice

1 **To make the gremolata,** finely chop the mint, parsley, garlic and lemon strips, then combine well.

2 **Heat a chargrill pan** or barbecue plate to very hot. Lightly brush barbecue plate with 1 tablespoon of the oil.

3 **Cook the cutlets** over medium heat for about 2 minutes on each side, or until cooked to your liking. Remove the cutlets and cover to keep warm. Allow to rest while cooking the vegetables.

4 **Trim the ends** from the carrots and zucchini and, using a sharp vegetable peeler, peel the vegetables lengthways into ribbons.

5 **Heat the remaining oil** in a large saucepan, add the vegetables and toss over medium heat for 3–5 minutes, or until sautéed but still tender.

6 **Divide the lamb cutlets** among four serving plates, lightly sprinkle the cutlets with the gremolata and drizzle with the lemon juice. Serve immediately with the vegetable ribbons.

CHICKEN FALAFEL WITH TABOULEH CONES

MAKES 24

45 g (1½ oz/¼ cup) burghul (bulgar)

4 pieces lavash or other unleavened bread (23 x 30 cm/9 x 12 inches)

2 spring onions (scallions), thinly sliced

1 large tomato, seeded and finely chopped

1 small Lebanese (short) cucumber, finely chopped

1 large handful flat-leaf (Italian) parsley, chopped

1 tablespoon lemon juice

1 tablespoon virgin olive oil

1 tablespoon olive oil

1 onion, finely chopped

1 garlic clove, crushed

2 teaspoons ground coriander

1 teaspoon cumin seeds

½ teaspoon ground cinnamon

250 g (9 oz) minced (ground) chicken

300 g (11 oz) tinned chickpeas, rinsed, drained and mashed

1 handful mint, chopped

1 handful flat-leaf (Italian) parsley, extra, chopped

2 tablespoons plain (all-purpose) flour

vegetable oil, for frying

60 g (2 oz/¼ cup) Greek-style yoghurt

1 Soak burghul in hot water for 20 minutes. Slice bread into thirds widthways, then cut in half. Keep bread covered with a damp cloth to prevent it drying out. Cut 24 pieces of baking paper the same size as the bread. Roll the paper up around the bottom half of the bread to form a cone and secure. Twist at the bottom. You will need 24 bread cones.

2 To make the tabouleh, drain the burghul in a fine mesh sieve, pressing out as much water as possible. Transfer to a bowl and mix with the spring onion, tomato, cucumber, parsley, lemon juice and virgin olive oil, and season.

3 Heat the olive oil in a frying pan, add the onion and garlic and cook, stirring over medium–low heat, for 5 minutes, or until the onion is soft. Add the spices and cook for another minute, or until the spices are aromatic.

4 Put the onion mixture, minced chicken, chickpeas, mint and extra parsley in a bowl, season and mix until combined. Shape into 24 firm falafel patties. Toss the falafel in the flour and shake off the excess.

5 Fill a deep-fryer or heavy-based saucepan one-third full of oil and heat to 180°C (350°F), or until a cube of bread dropped into the oil turns golden brown in 15 seconds. Cook falafels in batches for 3–4 minutes each side, or until golden and heated through. Drain on crumpled paper towels.

6 To assemble, put a falafel in each bread cone, top with tabouleh, then ½ teaspoon yoghurt.

Note: Tabouleh is best made on the day of serving, while the falafel can be prepared up to a day ahead and cooked just before serving.

SERVES 4

185 ml (6 fl oz/¾ cup) olive oil

2 tablespoons lime juice

4 garlic cloves, chopped

3 red chillies, chopped

2 tablespoons tequila (optional)

1 kg (2 lb 4 oz) rump steak, thinly sliced into strips

1 red and yellow capsicum (pepper), thinly sliced

1 red onion, thinly sliced

8 flour tortillas

ready-made guacamole, shredded lettuce, diced tomato and sour cream, to serve

1 Combine the oil, lime juice, garlic, chilli, tequila and some pepper in a large bowl. Add the meat, cover and marinate it for at least 1 hour or overnight in the refrigerator.

2 Drain the meat and toss it with the capsicum and onion.

3 Just before serving, wrap the tortillas in foil and warm them in a 150°C (300°F/Gas 2) oven for about 5 minutes.

4 Cook the meat and vegetables in batches in a sizzling-hot heavy-based frying pan until cooked.

5 Scoop onto a large serving plate and place in the middle of the table. Serve the tortillas, guacamole, shredded lettuce, diced tomato and sour cream in separate bowls or plates at the table and let everyone assemble their own fajita.

PORK CHOPS WITH APPLES AND CIDER

SERVES 4

1 tablespoon oil

2 onions, sliced

2 golden delicious apples, cored and cut into wedges

2 teaspoons caster (superfine) sugar

2 teaspoons butter

4 thick pork chops, snipped around the edges

3 tablespoons cider

3 tablespoons cream

1 Heat the oil in a large non-stick frying pan, add the onion and fry for about 5 minutes, or until soft and just beginning to brown. Tip the onion out onto a plate.

2 Add apple wedges to the pan. Fry for a minute or two — they should not break up, but will gradually start to soften and brown. Add the sugar and butter and shake everything around in the pan over the heat until the apples start to caramelize. Transfer the apples to the plate with the onion.

3 Put the pork chops in the frying pan, add a little seasoning and fry them for about 4 minutes on each side, or until they are cooked through. Put the onion and apple back in the pan and heat them up, then add the cider and bring to a simmer. Once the liquid is bubbling, add the cream and shake the pan so everything is well combined. Let it bubble for a minute, then season well.

4 Serve with potatoes and a green salad — watercress goes particularly well.

CHICKEN BREASTS WITH MUSTARD CREAM SAUCE

SERVES 4

4 chicken breasts (about 200 g/7 oz each)

2 tablespoons oil

1 garlic clove, crushed

3 tablespoons dry white wine

2 tablespoons wholegrain mustard

2 teaspoons chopped fresh thyme

300 ml (10½ fl oz) cream

250 g (9 oz) green beans, topped and tailed

320 g (11¼ oz) baby yellow squash, halved

1 **Pound each** chicken breast between sheets of plastic wrap with a mallet or rolling pin until about 1 cm (½ inch) thick.

2 **Heat the oil** in a frying pan over high heat. Brown the chicken breasts for 4–5 minutes on each side, or until brown. Remove and cover with foil.

3 **Add the garlic** to the frying pan and cook for 1 minute over medium heat, then stir in the wine, mustard and thyme. Increase the heat to medium–high and pour in the cream. Simmer for about 5 minutes, or until the sauce has reduced and thickened slightly, then season to taste.

4 **Meanwhile,** bring a saucepan of lightly salted water to the boil, add the beans and squash and cook for 2–4 minutes, or until just tender. Season to taste. To serve, pour a little of sauce over the chicken. Serve with the vegetables on the side.

CHINESE BEEF AND ASPARAGUS WITH OYSTER SAUCE

SERVES 4

500 g (1 lb 2 oz) lean beef fillet, thinly sliced across the grain

1 tablespoon light soy sauce

½ teaspoon sesame oil

1 tablespoon Chinese rice wine

2½ tablespoons vegetable oil

200 g (7 oz) fresh thin asparagus, cut into thirds on the diagonal

3 garlic cloves, crushed

2 teaspoons fresh ginger (cut into thin matchsticks)

3 tablespoons chicken stock

2–3 tablespoons oyster sauce

1 **Place the beef** slices in a non-metallic bowl with the soy sauce, sesame oil and 2 teaspoons of the rice wine. Cover and marinate for at least 15 minutes.

2 **Heat a wok** over high heat, add about 1 tablespoon of the vegetable oil and swirl to coat the side of the wok. When the oil is hot but not smoking, add the asparagus and stir-fry for 1–2 minutes. Remove from the wok.

3 **Add another** tablespoon of oil to the wok and, when hot, add the beef in two batches, stir-frying each batch for 1–2 minutes, or until cooked. Remove the meat from the wok.

4 **Add the remaining** oil to the wok and, when hot, add the garlic and ginger and stir-fry for 1 minute, or until fragrant. Pour the stock, oyster sauce and remaining rice wine into the wok, bring to the boil and boil rapidly for 1–2 minutes, or until the sauce is slightly reduced. Return the beef and asparagus to the wok and stir-fry for a further minute, or until heated through and coated in the sauce. Serve with steamed rice.

PORK WITH SWEET AND SOUR SAUCE

SERVES 4

225 g (8 oz) tinned pineapple slices
in light syrup, each slice cut into
4 pieces (reserve the syrup)

1½ tablespoons plum sauce or tomato
ketchup

2½ teaspoons fish sauce

1 tablespoon sugar

2 tablespoons vegetable oil

250 g (9 oz) pork, sliced

4 garlic cloves, finely chopped

¼ carrot, sliced

1 onion, cut into 8 slices

½ red capsicum (pepper), cut into
bite-sized pieces

1 small cucumber, unpeeled, halved
lengthways and cut into thick slices

1 tomato, cut into 4 slices, or 4–5 baby
tomatoes

a few coriander (cilantro) leaves, to
garnish

1 Mix the pineapple syrup (you will need 6 tablespoons) with the plum sauce, fish sauce and sugar in a small bowl until sugar has dissolved.

2 Heat the oil in a wok or deep frying pan over a medium heat and fry the pork until nicely browned and cooked. Lift out with a slotted spoon and drain on paper towels

3 Add the garlic to the wok or pan and fry over a medium heat for 1 minute or until lightly browned. Add the carrot, onion and capsicum and stir-fry for 1–2 minutes. Add the cucumber, tomato, pineapple and pineapple syrup and stir together for another minute. Taste, then adjust the seasoning.

4 Return the pork to the pan and gently stir. Spoon onto a serving plate and garnish with coriander leaves.

PARMESAN CHICKEN WITH QUICK SALSA VERDE

SERVES 4

3 eggs

1 large handful basil

2 tablespoons capers, rinsed

1 tablespoon dijon mustard

2 tablespoons freshly grated parmesan cheese

185 ml (6 fl oz/¾ cup) olive oil

100 g (4 oz/1 cup) dry breadcrumbs

4 boneless, skinless chicken breasts (about 120 g/4 oz each)

150 g (6 oz) rocket (arugula) leaves

lemon wedges, to serve

1 Place **1 egg** in a saucepan of cold water, bring to the boil and cook for 1 minute. Remove from the heat and refresh under cold water. Peel, then place in a food processor with the basil, capers, mustard and 1 tablespoon of the parmesan, until combined. Gradually add 3 tablespoons of the olive oil and process until you have a coarse sauce, taking care not to overprocess.

2 Beat remaining eggs together with 1 tablespoon water. Combine the breadcrumbs with the remaining parmesan on a plate. Pound each chicken breast between two sheets of plastic wrap with a mallet or rolling pin until 5 mm (¼ inch) thick. Dip the chicken in the egg mixture, then coat in the breadcrumb mixture. Place on a paper-lined baking tray and refrigerate for 10 minutes, or until needed.

3 Heat the remaining oil in a large frying pan over high heat. Cook the chicken breasts in batches for 2–3 minutes each batch, or until golden on both sides and cooked through — keep each batch warm. Serve with the salsa verde, rocket leaves and lemon wedges.

CHICKEN KARAAGE

MAKES 20 PIECES

1.5 kg (3 lb 5 oz) chicken

125 ml (4 fl oz/½ cup) Japanese soy sauce

60 ml (2 fl oz/¼ cup) mirin

2 tablespoons sake

1 tablespoon finely chopped fresh ginger

4 garlic cloves, crushed

oil, for deep-frying

cornflour (cornstarch), to coat

lemon wedges, to serve

1 **Using a cleaver** or a large kitchen knife, remove the wings from the chicken and chop them in half across the joint. Cut the chicken into 16 even-sized pieces by cutting it in half down the centre, then across each half to form four even pieces. Cut each quarter into four pieces, trying to retain some skin on each piece. You should have 20 pieces in total, including the four wing pieces.

2 **Combine the soy sauce,** mirin, sake, ginger and garlic in a large non-metallic bowl. Add the chicken and toss to coat well. Cover and refrigerate overnight, turning occasionally to evenly coat the chicken in the marinade.

3 **Preheat the oven** to 150°C (300°F/Gas 2). Fill a wok or deep heavy-based saucepan one-third full with oil and heat to 180°C (350°F), or until a cube of bread dropped into the oil browns in 15 seconds. While the oil is heating, drain the chicken and coat thoroughly in well-seasoned cornflour, shaking lightly to remove any excess.

4 **Deep-fry the chicken,** in batches, for 4–5 minutes, or until crisp and golden and the chicken is just cooked through and tender. Drain well on crumpled paper towel. Keep the cooked chicken warm in the oven while you cook the remainder. Serve hot with lemon wedges.

PEPPER STEAK

SERVES 4

4 x 200 g (7 oz) fillet steaks

2 tablespoons oil

6 tablespoons black peppercorns, crushed

40 g (1½ oz) butter

3 tablespoons Cognac or brandy

125 ml (4 fl oz/½ cup) thick (double/ heavy) cream

green salad, to serve

1 Rub the steaks on both sides with the oil and press the crushed peppercorns into the meat so they don't come off while you're frying. Melt the butter in a large frying pan and cook the steaks for 2–4 minutes on each side, depending on how you like your steak.

2 Add the Cognac or brandy and flambé by lighting the pan with your gas flame or a match (stand well back when you do this and keep a pan lid handy for emergencies). Lift the steaks out onto a warm plate.

3 Add the wine to the pan and boil, stirring, for 1 minute to deglaze the pan. Add the cream and stir for a couple of minutes. Season with salt and freshly ground black pepper and pour over the steaks. Serve with green salad.

HERBED LAMB CUTLETS WITH PRESERVED LEMON

SERVES 4

2 tablespoons finely chopped thyme
   leaves

2 teaspoons freshly ground black
   pepper

12 French-trimmed lamb cutlets

3 tablespoons virgin olive oil

2 tablespoons soy sauce

2 garlic cloves, crushed

oil, for brushing

PRESERVED LEMON COUSCOUS

1 tablespoon olive oil

185 g (6½ oz/1 cup) couscous

2 tablespoons thinly sliced preserved
   lemon zest

1 Sprinkle the thyme and pepper onto a plate. Use the mixture to coat both sides of each lamb cutlet, pressing it in well.

2 In a shallow non-metallic dish, whisk the oil, soy sauce and garlic until combined. Add the lamb cutlets, then cover and refrigerate for 20 minutes, turning once.

3 Preheat a barbecue grill plate or chargrill pan until very hot. Meanwhile, make the preserved lemon couscous.

4 Bring 375 ml (13 fl oz/1½ cups) of water to the boil in a saucepan. Add the oil, then stir in the couscous and preserved lemon. Remove from the heat, cover and leave for 5 minutes. Before serving, fluff up the couscous with a fork.

5 Shake the excess marinade off the cutlets and set them slightly apart on the barbecue hotplate. Grill for 1–2 minutes on each side, or until cooked to your liking. Serve the cutlets with the preserved lemon couscous.

MOROCCAN CHICKEN

SERVES 4

1 tablespoon ras el hanout (Moroccan spice blend)

800 g (1 lb 12 oz) boneless, skinless chicken thighs, trimmed and halved

1 tablespoon oil

60 g (2 oz) butter

1 large onion, cut into wedges

1 cinnamon stick

2 garlic cloves, crushed

2 tablespoons lemon juice

250 ml (9 fl oz/1 cup) chicken stock

75 g (3 oz/⅓ cup) pitted prunes, halved

225 g (8 oz/1½ cups) couscous

lemon wedges, to serve

1 **Sprinkle half the** spice blend over the chicken. Heat the oil and 20 g (1 oz) of the butter in a large saucepan or deep-sided frying pan over medium heat. Cook the chicken in two batches for 5 minutes, or until evenly browned. Remove from the pan, then add the onion and cinnamon stick and cook for 2–3 minutes before adding the garlic. Return the chicken to the pan and add the lemon juice and the remaining spice blend. Season, then cook, covered, for 5 minutes.

2 **Add the stock** and prunes to the pan and bring to the boil. Reduce the heat to medium–low and cook, uncovered, for 15 minutes, or until the chicken is cooked and the liquid has reduced to a sauce. Before serving, stir 20 g (1 oz) of the butter into the sauce.

3 **About 10 minutes** before the chicken is ready, place the couscous in a heatproof bowl, add 375 ml (13 fl oz/1½ cups) boiling water, and stand for 3–5 minutes. Stir in the remaining butter and fluff with a fork until the butter has melted and the grains separate. Serve with the chicken.

GREEK-STYLE LAMB

SERVES 4

400 g (14 oz) lean lamb fillets

olive oil spray

1 teaspoon olive oil

1 large red onion, sliced

3 zucchini (courgettes), thinly sliced

200 g (7 oz) cherry tomatoes, halved

3 garlic cloves, crushed

60 g (2 oz/½ cup) pitted black olives in brine, drained and cut in half

2 tablespoons lemon juice

2 tablespoons finely chopped oregano

100 g (4 oz) low-fat feta cheese, crumbled

50 g (2 oz/⅓ cup) pine nuts, lightly toasted

4 wholegrain bread rolls or stone-ground wholemeal pitta bread pockets, warmed

1 Trim the lamb, then cut across the grain into thin strips. Heat a large frying pan until hot and spray with the oil. Add the lamb in small batches and cook each batch over high heat for 1–2 minutes, or until browned. Remove all the lamb from the pan.

2 Heat the oil in the pan, then add the onion and zucchini. Cook, stirring, over high heat for 2 minutes, or until just tender. Add the cherry tomatoes and garlic. Cook for 1–2 minutes, or until the tomatoes have just softened. Return the meat to the pan and stir over high heat until heated through.

3 Remove the pan from the heat. Add the olives, lemon juice and oregano and toss until well combined.

4 Sprinkle with crumbled feta cheese and pine nuts before serving. Serve with the bread rolls or pitta bread pockets and a mixed green salad, if desired.

FILLET STEAK WITH FLAVOURED BUTTERS

SERVES 4

4 fillet steaks

CAPSICUM BUTTER

1 small red capsicum (pepper)

125 g (5 oz) butter

2 teaspoons chopped oregano

2 teaspoons snipped chives

GARLIC BUTTER

125 g (5 oz) butter

3 garlic cloves, crushed

2 spring onions (scallions), finely chopped

1 Cut a pocket in each steak.

2 For the capsicum butter, cut the capsicum into large pieces and place, skin side up, under a hot grill (broiler) until the skin blisters and blackens. Put in a plastic bag until cool, then peel away the skin and dice the flesh.

3 Beat the butter until creamy. Add the capsicum, oregano and chives, season and beat until smooth.

4 For the garlic butter, beat the butter until creamy, add the garlic and spring onion and beat until smooth.

5 Push capsicum butter into the pockets in two of the steaks and garlic butter into the other two.

6 Cook on a hot, lightly oiled barbecue grill or flat plate for 4–5 minutes each side, turning once. Brush with any remaining flavoured butter while cooking. These steaks are delicious served with a green salad.

LIME AND CORIANDER CHARGRILLED CHICKEN

SERVES 4

3 teaspoons finely grated fresh ginger

25 g (1 oz) chopped coriander (cilantro) leaves

1½ teaspoons grated lime zest

4 tablespoons lime juice

4 skinless chicken breast fillets (about 750 g/1lb 10 oz), trimmed

250 g (9 oz/1¼ cups) jasmine rice

2 tablespoons oil

3 zucchini (courgettes), cut into wedges

4 large flat mushrooms, stalks trimmed

1 **Combine the ginger,** coriander, lime zest and 2 tablespoons of the lime juice. Spread 2 teaspoons of the herb mixture over each chicken breast and season well. Marinate for 1 hour. Combine the remaining herb mixture with the remaining lime juice in a screwtop jar. Set aside until needed.

2 **Bring a large saucepan** of water to the boil. Add the rice and cook for 12 minutes, stirring occasionally. Drain well.

3 **Meanwhile,** heat a barbecue plate to medium and lightly brush with oil. Brush the zucchini and mushrooms with the remaining oil. Place the chicken on the chargrill plate and cook on each side for 4–5 minutes, or until cooked through. Add the vegetables during the last 5 minutes of cooking, and turn frequently until browned on the outside and just softened. Cover with foil until ready to serve.

4 **Divide the rice** among four bowls. Cut the chicken fillets into long thick strips, then arrange on top of the rice. Shake the dressing well and drizzle over the chicken and serve with the chargrilled vegetables.

STICKY PORK FILLET

SERVES 4

3 tablespoons Chinese rice wine

3 tablespoons char siu sauce

2 tablespoons hoisin sauce

1 tablespoon honey

3 garlic cloves, finely chopped

1 tablespoon finely grated fresh ginger

1 teaspoon Chinese five spice

1 teaspoon sesame oil

2 x 300 g (10½ oz) pork fillets, cut in half

400 g (14 oz) baby bok choy (pak choy), halved and rinsed

1 **Combine the rice wine,** sauces, honey, garlic, ginger, five spice and sesame oil in a shallow dish. Add the pork and toss until well coated. Cover and leave to marinate in the refrigerator.

2 **Line the bottom** basket of a double steamer with several pieces of baking paper and the top basket with a single layer. Punch the paper with holes. Lay the pork in a single layer in the bottom basket and cover with a lid. Sit the steamer over a wok or saucepan of boiling water and steam for 20 minutes, basting the pork regularly.

3 **Lay the bok choy** in the top steamer basket, cover and steam both baskets for a further 5 minutes. Remove the pork and cover. Pour the remaining marinade into a small saucepan, stir in 1–2 tablespoons of water and simmer over high heat for 5 minutes to reduce slightly.

4 **Slice the pork fillets** and arrange on plates or in bowls with the bok choy. Drizzle with the sauce and serve with steamed rice.

MONGOLIAN LAMB

SERVES 4–6

2 garlic cloves, crushed
2 teaspoons finely grated fresh ginger
3 tablespoons Chinese rice wine
3 tablespoons soy sauce
2 tablespoons hoisin sauce
1 teaspoon sesame oil
1 kg (2 lb 4 oz) lamb loin fillets, thinly sliced across the grain
4 tablespoons peanut oil
6 spring onions (scallions), cut into 3 cm (1¼ inch) lengths
2 teaspoons chilli sauce
1½ tablespoons hoisin sauce, extra

1 **Combine the garlic,** ginger, Chinese rice wine, soy sauce, hoisin sauce and sesame oil in a large non-metallic bowl. Add the lamb and toss until well coated. Cover with plastic wrap and marinate in the refrigerator overnight, tossing occasionally.

2 **Heat a wok** over high heat, add about 1 tablespoon of the peanut oil and swirl to coat the wok. Add the spring onion and stir-fry for 1 minute, or until lightly golden. Remove, reserving the oil in the wok.

3 **Lift the lamb** out of the marinade with tongs, reserving the marinade. Add the meat in four batches and stir-fry for about 1–2 minutes per batch, or until browned but not completely cooked through, adding more oil and making sure the wok is very hot before cooking each batch. Return all the meat and any juices to the wok with the spring onion and stir-fry for 1 minute, or until meat is cooked through.

4 **Remove the meat** and spring onion from the wok with a slotted spoon and place in a serving bowl, retaining the liquid in the wok. Add any reserved marinade to the wok along with the chilli sauce and extra hoisin sauce, then boil for about 4 minutes, or until the sauce thickens and becomes slightly syrupy. Spoon the sauce over the lamb, toss together well, then serve with steamed rice.

CHICKEN WITH ALMONDS AND ASPARAGUS

SERVES 4–6

2 teaspoons cornflour (cornstarch)

80 ml (3 fl oz/⅓ cup) chicken stock

¼ teaspoon sesame oil

2 tablespoons oyster sauce

1 tablespoon soy sauce

3 garlic cloves, crushed

1 teaspoon finely chopped fresh ginger

pinch ground white pepper

2½ tablespoons peanut oil

50 g (2 oz/⅓ cup) blanched almonds

2 spring onions (scallions), cut into 3 cm (1¼ inch) lengths

500 g (1 lb 2 oz) boneless, skinless chicken thighs, cut into thin strips

1 small carrot, thinly sliced

155 g (6 oz) asparagus, trimmed and cut into 3 cm (1¼ inch) lengths

60 g (2 oz/¼ cup) tinned bamboo shoots, sliced

steamed rice, to serve

1 **To make the stir-fry sauce,** put cornflour and stock in a small bowl and mix to form a paste, then stir in the sesame oil, oyster sauce, soy sauce, garlic, ginger and white pepper. Set aside until needed.

2 **Heat a wok** over high heat, add 2 teaspoons of the peanut oil and swirl to coat the base and side. Add the almonds and stir-fry for 1–2 minutes, or until golden — be careful not to burn them. Remove from the wok and drain on crumpled paper towel.

3 **Heat another teaspoon** of the peanut oil in the wok and swirl to coat. Add the spring onion and stir-fry for 30 seconds, or until wilted. Remove from the wok and set aside.

4 **Heat 1 tablespoon** of the peanut oil in the wok over high heat, add the chicken in two batches and stir-fry for 3 minutes, or until the chicken is just cooked through. Set aside with the spring onion.

5 **Add remaining** peanut oil to the wok, then add the carrot and stir-fry for 1–2 minutes, or until just starting to brown. Toss in the asparagus and the bamboo shoots and stir-fry for a further 1 minute. Remove all the vegetables from the wok and set aside with the chicken and spring onion.

6 **Stir the stir-fry sauce** briefly, then pour into the wok, stirring until the mixture thickens. Return the chicken and vegetables to the wok and stir thoroughly for a couple of minutes until they are coated in the sauce and are heated through. Transfer to a serving dish and sprinkle with the almonds before serving. Serve with steamed rice.

FIVE-SPICE PORK STIR-FRY

SERVES 4

375 g (13 oz) fresh thin egg noodles
1 tablespoon sesame oil
3 teaspoons grated fresh ginger
1½ teaspoons Chinese five-spice
2 teaspoons rice flour
500 g (1 lb 2 oz) pork loin fillet, thinly sliced across the grain
2 tablespoons vegetable oil
2 garlic cloves, crushed
1 red capsicum (pepper), thinly sliced
300 g (11 oz) bok choy (pak choy), chopped
6 spring onions (scallions), sliced
2 tablespoons Chinese rice wine
2 tablespoons hoisin sauce
1 tablespoon soy sauce

1 **Cook the noodles** in a saucepan of boiling water for 1 minute. Drain, rinse and return to the saucepan. Stir in half of the sesame oil. Set aside.

2 **Place the ginger,** five-spice and rice flour in a bowl, season, then mix well. Add the pork and toss to coat.

3 **Heat a wok** over high heat, add half of the vegetable oil and swirl to coat the base and side. Add the pork in batches and stir-fry for 5 minutes at a time, or until tender. Remove from the wok and set aside. Add the remaining vegetable oil, garlic, capsicum, bok choy and spring onion and stir-fry for 3 minutes, or until softened.

4 **Return the pork** to the wok and stir in the rice wine, hoisin sauce, soy sauce and the remaining sesame oil and simmer for 2 minutes. Add the noodles and reheat gently before serving.

THAI BEEF SKEWERS WITH PEANUT SAUCE

SERVES 4

1 onion, chopped

2 garlic cloves, crushed

2 teaspoons sambal oelek

1 lemongrass stem, white part only, chopped

2 teaspoons chopped fresh ginger

1½ tablespoons oil

270 ml (9½ fl oz) coconut cream

125 g (5 oz/½ cup) crunchy peanut butter

1½ tablespoons fish sauce

2 teaspoons soy sauce

1 tablespoon grated palm (jaggery) sugar or soft brown sugar

2 tablespoons lime juice

2 tablespoons chopped coriander (cilantro) leaves

750 g (1 lb 10 oz) round or rump steak, cut into 2 cm x 10 cm (¾ x 4 inches) pieces

2 teaspoons oil, extra

fresh red chilli, chopped, to garnish (optional)

chopped roasted peanuts, to garnish (optional)

1 **Put the onion,** garlic, sambal oelek, lemongrass and ginger in a food processor and process to a smooth paste.

2 **Heat the oil** in a saucepan over medium heat, add paste and cook, stirring, for 2–3 minutes, or until fragrant. Add the coconut cream, peanut butter, fish sauce, soy sauce, sugar and lime juice and bring to the boil. Reduce the heat and simmer for 5 minutes, then stir in the coriander.

3 **Meanwhile,** thread the meat onto 12 metal skewers, and cook on a hot chargrill or in a non-stick frying pan with the extra oil for 2 minutes each side, or until cooked to your liking. Serve the skewers on a bed of rice with the sauce and a salad on the side. Garnish with chopped chilli and peanuts,.

Note: If using wooden skewers, soak them for 30 minutes before grilling to prevent them from burning.

FRIED CRISPY CHICKEN

SERVES 4

4 chicken leg quarters or 8 drumsticks

4 garlic cloves, chopped

3 coriander (cilantro) roots, finely chopped

2 teaspoons ground turmeric

1 teaspoon caster (superfine) sugar

2 tablespoons chilli sauce, plus extra to serve

oil, for deep-frying

1 Remove the skin from the chicken pieces. Put the chicken in a large saucepan with enough water to cover it. Cover and simmer for 15 minutes, or until cooked through. Drain and allow to cool.

2 Put the garlic, coriander root, turmeric, 1 teaspoon pepper, 1 teaspoon salt, sugar and chilli sauce in a mortar and pestle or food processor and pound or process into a smooth paste. Brush over the chicken, coating it thoroughly. Cover and refrigerate for 30 minutes.

3 Heat the oil in a heavy-based frying pan, add the chicken in batches and cook until dark brown, turning frequently. Drain on paper towels. Serve hot or cold with chilli sauce.

GARLIC PORK CHOPS

SERVES 4

1 kg (2 lb 4 oz) pork chops

8 garlic cloves, crushed

2 tablespoons fish sauce

1 tablespoon soy sauce

2 tablespoons oyster sauce

2 tablespoons chopped spring onion (scallion)

1 **Put the pork chops** in a large glass bowl and add the garlic, fish sauce, soy sauce, oyster sauce and ½ teaspoon freshly ground black pepper. Stir well so that all the meat is covered with the marinade. Cover and marinate in the refrigerator for 4 hours.

2 **Heat a barbecue grill** or hotplate to hot and cook the pork on all sides until browned and cooked through. Alternatively you can cook the pork under a hot grill (broiler). If the pork starts to burn, move it further away from the grill element.

3 **Arrange the pork** on a serving platter and scatter over the spring onion.

RACK OF LAMB WITH HERB CRUST

SERVES 4

2 x 6–rib racks of lamb, French-trimmed

1 tablespoon oil

80 g (3 oz/1 cup) fresh breadcrumbs

3 garlic cloves

3 tablespoons finely chopped flat-leaf (Italian) parsley

2 teapoons thyme leaves

½ teaspoon finely grated lemon zest

60 g (2 oz) butter, softened

250 ml (9 fl oz/1 cup) beef stock

1 garlic clove, extra, finely chopped

1 thyme sprig

1 **Preheat the oven** to 250°C (500°F/Gas 9). Score the fat on the lamb racks in a diamond pattern. Rub with a little oil and season.

2 **Heat the oil** in a frying pan over high heat, add the lamb racks and brown for 4–5 minutes. Remove and set aside. Do not wash the pan as you will need it later.

3 **In a large bowl,** mix the breadcrumbs, garlic, parsley, thyme leaves and lemon zest. Season, then mix in the butter to form a smooth paste.

4 **Firmly press** a layer of breadcrumb mixture over the fat on the lamb racks, leaving the bones and base clean. Bake in a roasting tin for 12 minutes for medium–rare. Rest the lamb on a plate while you make the jus.

5 **To make the jus,** add the beef stock, extra garlic and thyme sprig to the roasting tin juices, scraping the pan. Return this liquid to the original frying pan and simmer over high heat for 5–8 minutes, or until the sauce has reduced. Strain and serve with the lamb.

SPICY CHICKEN BURGERS

SERVES 4

500 g (1 lb 2 oz) lean minced (ground) chicken

4 spring onions (scallions), finely chopped

4 tablespoons chopped coriander (cilantro) leaves

2 garlic cloves, crushed

¼ teaspoon cayenne pepper

1 egg white, lightly beaten

1 tablespoon olive or canola oil

1 lemon, halved

150 g (6 oz) tabouleh

4 wholegrain bread rolls, halved

1 **Combine the chicken,** spring onion, coriander, garlic, cayenne pepper and egg white and season with salt and freshly ground black pepper. Shape the mixture into four patties. Refrigerate for 20 minutes before cooking.

2 **Heat the oil** in a large non-stick frying pan over medium heat. Add the patties and cook for about 5 minutes on each side, or until browned and cooked through.

3 **Squeeze lemon** on the cooked patties and drain well on crumpled paper towels. Add patties to the halved wholegrain buns and fill with the tabouleh. Serve with a green salad and some chilli sauce.

HAMBURGERS WITH FRESH CORN RELISH

SERVES 4

700 g (1 lb 9 oz) minced (ground) beef
1 garlic clove
2 small onions, very finely chopped
2 tablespoons parsley, finely chopped
1 tablespoon tomato ketchup
¼ teaspoon worcestershire sauce
2 corn cobs
2 tomatoes, finely chopped
1 tablespoon sweet chilli sauce
1 handful coriander (cilantro) leaves
lime juice
1 tablespoon oil
4 hamburger buns
baby cos (romaine) leaves, to serve

1 Turn on the grill (broiler). Put the beef in a bowl with the garlic, half of the onion, the parsley, tomato ketchup and the worcestershire sauce. Season and mix well, then leave it to marinate while you make the relish.

2 Grill the corn cobs on all sides until slightly blackened and charred around the edges. By this time the corn should be cooked through. Slice off the kernels by slicing down the length of each cob with a sharp knife. Mix the kernels with the tomato, chilli sauce, coriander and remaining onion. Add lime juice and salt and pepper, to taste.

3 Form the beef mixture into four large patties and flatten them out to the size of the buns (bear in mind that they will shrink as they cook).

4 Heat oil in a frying pan and fry the patties for 3–5 minutes on each side, depending on how well cooked you like them. While they are cooking, toast the buns.

5 Lay a lettuce leaf or two on each bun bottom, add some relish and top with a hamburger patty and the bun top, serving any extra relish on the side.

CHILLI PORK WITH CASHEWS

SERVES 4

2–3 tablespoons peanut oil

600 g (1 lb 5 oz) pork fillet, thinly sliced

4 spring onions (scallions), cut into 3 cm (1¼ inch) lengths

50 g (2 oz/⅓ cup) toasted unsalted cashews

1 tablespoon fish sauce

1 tablespoon mushroom oyster sauce

1–2 tablespoons Thai chilli paste in soy bean oil or chilli jam

1 large handful Thai basil leaves, plus extra to garnish

1 **Heat a wok** over high heat, add about 1 tablespoon of peanut oil and swirl to coat. Stir-fry the pork in batches for 2–3 minutes, or until it starts to brown. Remove from the wok and keep warm.

2 **Heat the remaining oil,** then stir-fry the spring onion for 1 minute. Return the pork to the wok, along with any juices, and stir-fry for 2 minutes.

3 **Stir in the cashews,** fish sauce, oyster sauce and chilli paste or jam. Toss for a further 2 minutes, or until the pork is tender and coated with the sauce.

4 **Remove from the heat** and gently stir in the Thai basil. Serve garnished with some extra basil.

LAMB, MINT AND CHILLI STIR-FRY

SERVES 4

250 g (9 oz/1¼ cups) jasmine rice

2 tablespoons oil

750 g (1 lb 10 oz) lamb backstrap or eye of loin fillets, sliced thinly

2 garlic cloves, finely chopped

1 small red onion, cut into wedges

1 fresh bird's eye chilli, finely chopped

3 tablespoons lime juice

2 tablespoons sweet chilli sauce

2 tablespoons fish sauce

1 handful fresh mint leaves

1 **Bring a large saucepan** of water to the boil. Add the rice and cook for 12 minutes, stirring occasionally. Drain well.

2 **Meanwhile,** heat a wok until very hot, add 1 tablespoon oil and swirl to coat. Add the lamb in batches and cook for 2 minutes, or until browned. Remove from the wok.

3 **Heat the remaining oil** in the wok, add the garlic and onion and stir-fry for 1 minute, then add the chilli and cook for 30 seconds. Return lamb to the wok, then add the lime juice, sweet chilli sauce and fish sauce and stir-fry for 2 minutes over high heat. Stir in the mint and serve with the rice.

Note: You can use chicken breasts or pork loin, adding 80 g (3 oz/½ cup) cashews and using basil instead of mint.

FRIED BEEF WITH POTATO, PEAS AND GINGER

SERVES 4

oil, for deep-frying

1 potato, cut into small cubes

2.5 cm (1 inch) piece of ginger

500 g (1 lb 2 oz) beef rump steak, thinly sliced

3 garlic cloves, crushed

1 teaspoon ground black pepper

2 tablespoons oil, extra

2 onions, sliced in rings

3 tablespoons beef stock

2 tablespoons tomato paste (concentrated purée)

½ tablespoon soy sauce

1 teaspoon chilli powder

3 tablespoons lemon juice

3 tomatoes, chopped

50 g (2 oz/⅓ cup) fresh or frozen peas

1 **Fill a deep heavy-based saucepan** one-third full with oil and heat to 180°C (350°F), or until a cube of bread dropped in the oil browns in 15 seconds. Deep-fry the potato cubes until golden brown. Drain on paper towels.

2 **Pound the ginger** using a mortar and pestle, or grate with a fine grater into a bowl. Put the ginger into a piece of muslin, twist it up tightly and squeeze out all the juice (you will need about 1 tablespoon).

3 **Put the steak** in a bowl, add the garlic, pepper and ginger juice and toss well. Heat the oil and fry the beef quickly in batches over high heat. Keep each batch warm as you remove it. Reduce the heat, then fry the onions until golden. Remove and set aside to keep warm.

4 **Put the stock,** tomato paste, soy sauce, chilli powder and lemon juice in the saucepan and cook over medium heat until reduced. Add the fried onion, cook for 3 minutes, add the chopped tomato and the peas, then stir well and cook for 1 minute. Add the beef and potato and toss well until heated through. Serve immediately.

FIVE-SPICE PORK RIBS

SERVES 4

1 kg (2 lb 4 oz) American-style pork ribs

shredded spring onions (scallions),
to serve

MARINADE

125 ml (4 fl oz/½ cup) tomato sauce
(ketchup)

2 tablespoons Chinese rice wine or dry
sherry

2 tablespoons light soy sauce

2 tablespoons honey

1 tablespoon sweet chilli sauce

2 teaspoons five-spice

2 garlic cloves, crushed

1 Slice the pork ribs into individual ribs. Combine the marinade ingredients in a non-metallic bowl. Add the ribs and toss well to coat. Cover and marinate in the refrigerator for several hours.

2 Preheat the oven to 180°C (350°F/Gas 4). Line a large baking tray with foil.

3 Remove excess marinade from the ribs, reserving it for basting when cooking.

4 Put the ribs on a rack on the baking tray. Bake for about 30 minutes, or until cooked and golden brown.

5 Brush with the reserved marinade once or twice during cooking. Serve the ribs hot and generously garnish with spring onions if desired.

GLAZED HOISIN CHICKEN STIR-FRY

SERVES 4

½ teaspoon sesame oil

1 egg white

1 tablespoon cornflour (cornstarch)

700 g (1 lb 9 oz) boneless, skinless chicken thighs, cut into small cubes

2 tablespoons peanut oil

2 garlic cloves, chopped

1 tablespoon finely shredded fresh ginger

1 tablespoon brown bean sauce

1 tablespoon hoisin sauce

1 tablespoon Chinese rice wine

1 teaspoon light soy sauce

4 spring onions (scallions), finely sliced

steamed rice, to serve

1   Combine the sesame oil, egg white and cornflour in a large non-metallic bowl. Add the chicken, toss to coat in the marinade, then cover with plastic wrap and marinate in the refrigerator for at least 15 minutes.

2   Heat a wok over high heat, add the peanut oil and swirl to coat the base and side. Add the chicken in three batches and stir-fry for 4 minutes at a time, or until cooked through. Remove the chicken from the wok and set aside.

3   Reheat the wok over high heat, add a little extra oil if necessary, then add the garlic and ginger and stir-fry for 1 minute. Return the chicken to the wok and add the bean sauce and hoisin sauce and cook, stirring, for 1 minute. Add the rice wine, soy sauce and spring onion and cook for 1 minute, or until the sauce is thick and glossy and coats the chicken. Serve with steamed rice.

VEAL SCHNITZEL WITH DILL POTATO SALAD

SERVES 4

750 g (1 lb 10 oz) desiree potatoes, unpeeled
500 g (1 lb 2 oz) veal leg steaks
60 g (2 oz/½ cup) seasoned plain (all-purpose) flour
2 eggs, lightly beaten
100 g (4 oz/1 cup) dry breadcrumbs
125 ml (4 fl oz/½ cup) virgin olive oil
2 tablespoons lemon juice
1½ tablespoons finely chopped fresh dill
200 g (7 oz) mixed salad leaves

1 **Cook the potatoes** in a large saucepan of boiling water for 15–20 minutes, or until tender. Drain, then cut into quarters lengthways and cover to keep warm.

2 **Meanwhile,** beat the veal between two sheets of plastic wrap to 5 mm (¼ inch) thickness. Coat the veal in the flour and shake off the excess. Dip the veal in the egg, then coat in breadcrumbs. Place the schnitzel on a flat tray, cover and freeze for 5 minutes.

3 **Heat** 60 ml (2 fl oz/¼ cup) of the oil in a large frying pan and cook the veal in two batches, over medium–high heat for 2–3 minutes on each side, or until golden and cooked through. Drain on crumpled paper towels and keep warm.

4 **Whisk the lemon juice,** dill and remaining oil together in a small bowl and pour over the potatoes. Season with salt and freshly ground black pepper and toss gently. Serve the schnitzel with the potatoes and a mixed salad.

FILLET STEAKS WITH PINK PEPPERCORN SAUCE

SERVES 4

60 g (2 oz) butter

1 tablespoon oil

4 fillet steaks, rump or New York cut, trimmed

125 ml (4 fl oz/½ cup) white wine

2 tablespoons brandy

125 ml (4 fl oz/½ cup) beef stock

2 tablespoons pink peppercorns in brine, drained and rinsed

125 ml (4 fl oz/½ cup) cream

1 **Heat butter** and oil in a large frying pan, and cook steaks over high heat for 3–4 minutes each side, or until cooked to your liking. Remove from the pan, cover and keep warm.

2 **Add the wine** and brandy to the pan, and simmer for 4 minutes, or until reduced by half. Add beef stock and reduce by half again. You should have just over 125 ml (4 fl oz/½ cup) sauce. Meanwhile, roughly chop half the peppercorns.

3 **Stir in** all the peppercorns and the cream, and cook gently until the sauce has thickened slightly. Place the steaks on four warmed serving plates and spoon the sauce over the top. Serve with a green salad.

BEEF STROGANOFF

SERVES 4

600 g (1 lb 5 oz) rib eye fillet or rump

30 g (1 oz/¼ cup) seasoned plain (all-purpose) flour

375 g (13 oz) fettuccine or tagliatelle

60 g (2 oz) butter

1 small onion, finely chopped

300 g (11 oz) button mushrooms, thickly sliced

1 tablespoon tomato paste (tomato purée)

60 ml (2 fl oz/¼ cup) red wine

300 ml (10½ fl oz) cream

1 Pound the slices of beef between two sheets of plastic wrap with a mallet or rolling pin until half their thickness. Cut each slice into strips about 1 cm (½ inch) wide. Place in a plastic bag with the seasoned flour and shake to coat.

2 Cook the pasta in a large saucepan of rapidly boiling salted water until al dente.

3 Meanwhile, melt 40 g (1½ oz) of the butter in a frying pan over medium heat and cook the onion for 2 minutes. Add the beef in batches and cook for 5 minutes, or until evenly browned. Remove from the pan and keep warm.

4 Heat remaining butter in the pan. Add the mushrooms, stirring, for 2–3 minutes, or until soft and lightly browned. Add the tomato paste and red wine, stirring continuously for 2 minutes, or until the sauce has reduced. Add the beef, stir in the cream, then reduce the heat to medium–low and simmer gently for another minute, or until the sauce has thickened. Serve with the pasta.

TERIYAKI CHICKEN WITH GINGER CHIVE RICE

SERVES 4

4 small boneless chicken breasts, skin on (about 170 g (6 oz) each)

60 ml (2 fl oz/¼ cup) Japanese soy sauce

2 tablespoons sake

1½ tablespoons mirin

1½ tablespoons soft brown sugar

3 teaspoons finely grated fresh ginger

300 g (11 oz/1½ cups) long-grain rice

2 tablespoons finely snipped -fresh chives

2 tablespoons oil

1 Pound each breast between sheets of plastic wrap with a mallet until 1 cm (½ inch) thick. Put the soy sauce, sake, mirin, sugar and 1 teaspoon ginger in a flat non-metallic dish and stir until the sugar has dissolved. Add the chicken and turn to coat. Cover and refrigerate for 1 hour, turning once.

2 Bring a large saucepan of water to the boil. Add the rice and cook for 12 minutes, stirring occasionally. Drain. Stir in the chives and remaining ginger, then cover until ready to serve.

3 Drain the chicken, reserving the marinade. Heat the oil in a deep frying pan and cook the chicken, skin-side-down over medium heat for 5 minutes, until the skin is crisp. Turn and cook for 4 minutes (not quite cooked).

4 Add the marinade and 60 ml (2 fl oz/ ¼ cup) water to the pan and scrape up any sediment. Bring to the boil over high heat, then add the chicken (skin side up) and juices. Cook for 5–6 minutes, until cooked through, turning once. (If the sauce is runny, remove the chicken and boil the sauce until syrupy.) Serve the chicken whole or sliced, drizzled with the sauce.

SICHUAN CHICKEN

SERVES 4

¼ teaspoon Chinese five-spice

750 g (1 lb 10 oz) boneless, skinless chicken thighs, halved

2 tablespoons peanut oil

1 tablespoon julienned fresh ginger

1 teaspoon sichuan peppercorns, crushed

1 teaspoon chilli bean paste (toban jian)

2 tablespoons light soy sauce

1 tablespoon Chinese rice wine

250 g (9 oz/1¼ cups) jasmine rice

600 g (1 lb 5 oz) baby bok choy (pak choy), leaves separated

1 **Sprinkle the** five-spice over the chicken. Heat a saucepan or wok until very hot, add half the oil and swirl to coat. Add the chicken and cook for 2 minutes each side, or until browned. Remove from the pan or wok.

2 **Reduce the heat** to medium and cook the ginger for 30 seconds. Add the peppercorns and chilli bean paste.

3 **Return the chicken** to the pan or wok, add the soy sauce, wine and 125 ml (4 fl oz/½ cup) water, then simmer for about 15–20 minutes, or until cooked.

4 **Meanwhile,** add the rice to a large saucepan of rapidly boiling water and cook for 12 minutes, stirring occasionally. Drain well.

5 **Heat the remaining oil** in a large saucepan. Add the bok choy and toss for 1 minute, or until the leaves wilt and the stems are tender. Serve with the chicken and rice.

TANDOORI CHICKEN WITH CARDAMOM RICE

SERVES 4

200 g (7 oz/¾ cup) plain yoghurt, plus extra for serving

60 g (2 oz/¼ cup) good-quality tandoori paste

2 tablespoons lemon juice

1 kg (2 lb 4 oz) boneless, skinless chicken breasts, cut into 3 cm (1 inch) cubes

1 tablespoon oil

1 onion, finely diced

300 g (11 oz/1½ cups long-grain rice

2 cardamom pods, bruised

750 ml (27 fl oz/3 cups) hot chicken stock

400 g (14 oz) baby spinach leaves

1 Soak eight wooden skewers in water for 30 minutes to prevent them burning during cooking. Combine yoghurt, tandoori paste and lemon juice in a non-metallic dish. Add the chicken and coat well in the mixture. Cover and marinate for at least 10 minutes.

2 Meanwhile, heat the oil in a saucepan. Add onion and cook for 3 minutes, then add the rice and cardamom pods. Cook, stirring often, for 3–5 minutes, or until the rice is slightly opaque. Add stock and bring to the boil. Reduce the heat to low, cover, and cook, without removing the lid, for 15 minutes.

3 Meanwhile, heat a barbecue plate or oven grill to very hot. Thread the chicken cubes onto the skewers, leaving the bottom quarter of the skewers empty. Cook on each side for 4–5 minutes, or until cooked through.

4 Wash the spinach and place in a large saucepan with just the water clinging to the leaves. Cook, covered, over medium heat for 1–2 minutes, or until the spinach has wilted. Uncover the rice, fluff with a fork and serve with the spinach, chicken and extra yoghurt.

BEEF IN BLACK BEAN SAUCE

SERVES 4

4 tablespoons tinned salted black beans in soy sauce

750 g (1 lb 10 oz) rump steak

1 tablespoon peanut oil

1 tablespoon sesame oil

1 large onion, thinly sliced

1 garlic clove, finely chopped

2.5 cm (1 inch) piece of fresh ginger, peeled and finely chopped

1 small fresh red chilli, finely chopped

2 teaspoons cornflour (cornstarch)

2 tablespoons dark soy sauce

1 teaspoon sugar

60 ml (2 fl oz/¼ cup) beef stock

1 spring onion (scallions), thinly sliced on the diagonal, to garnish

1 **Rinse, then soak** black beans in cold water for 5 minutes. Drain and roughly mash beans with a fork. Trim the steak of all fat and sinew, then cut meat in thin slices across the grain.

2 **Heat a saucepan** over medium heat, add half each of the peanut and sesame oils. Add the beef in two batches, and stir each for 2 minutes, or until well browned. Transfer the beef and any liquid to a bowl. Heat the remaining oils, add the onion and stir for 2 minutes. Add the garlic, ginger and chilli, and stir for 1 minute.

3 **Mix cornflour** with 1 teaspoon water, then return the beef and any cooking liquid to the pan with the black beans, soy sauce, sugar, stock and cornflour paste. Stir for 1–2 minutes, or until the sauce boils and thickens. Garnish with the spring onions and serve with steamed rice.

VEAL SCALOPPINE WITH WHITE WINE AND PARSLEY

SERVES 4

4 x 170 g (6 oz) veal escalopes

30 g (1 oz) butter

60 ml (2 fl oz/¼ cup) dry white wine or dry Marsala (not sweet)

100 ml (4 fl oz) thick (double/heavy) cream

1 tablespoon wholegrain mustard

2 tablespoons chopped fresh flat-leaf (Italian) parsley

1 Place the veal escalopes between two sheets of plastic wrap and either press down hard with the heel of your hand until flattened, or flatten with a rolling pin or mallet. Heat the butter in a frying pan and cook the escalopes in batches for 1 minute each side, or until just cooked. Remove and cover.

2 Add the wine to the pan, bring to the boil and cook for 1–2 minutes, or until reduced by half. Then add the cream, bring to the boil and reduce by half again. Stir in the mustard and 1 tablespoon parsley until just combined.

3 Return the veal to the pan to warm through and coat in the sauce. Serve the veal with a little sauce and sprinkle with the remaining parsley. Serve with potatoes and a green salad.

SPRING ONION LAMB

SERVES 4

600 g (1 lb 5 oz) lean lamb backstraps or eye of loin fillets, sliced across the grain into very thin slices

1 tablespoon Chinese rice wine or dry sherry

60 ml (2 fl oz/¼ cup) soy sauce

½ teaspoon white pepper

6 spring onions (scallions)

300 g (11 oz/1½ cups) long-grain rice

2 tablespoons oil

750 g (11 oz/1½ cups) choy sum, cut into 10 cm (4 inch) lengths

3 garlic cloves, crushed

1 tablespoon Chinese black vinegar

1 teaspoon sesame oil

1 Put the lamb in a non-metallic bowl with the rice wine, 1 tablespoon soy sauce, ½ teaspoon salt and the white pepper and mix. Cover and chill for 10 minutes. Slice the spring onions diagonally into 4 cm (1½ inch) lengths.

2 Meanwhile, bring a large pan of water to the boil. Add the rice and cook for 12 minutes, stirring occasionally. Drain.

3 Heat a wok over high heat, add ½ tablespoon oil and swirl to coat. Add the choy sum, stir-fry, then add 1 garlic clove and 1 tablespoon soy sauce. Cook for 3 minutes, or until crisp, then take the wok off the heat, remove the greens and keep warm.

4 Wipe out wok and heat over high heat. Add 1 tablespoon oil and swirl. Add the lamb in batches and stir-fry over high heat for 1–2 minutes, or until brown. Remove from the wok.

5 Add more oil to the wok if necessary. Add spring onion and remaining garlic and stir-fry for 1–2 minutes. Combine the vinegar, sesame oil and the remaining soy sauce. Pour into the wok, stirring for 1 minute. Return the lamb to the wok and stir-fry for another minute, or until combined and heated through. Serve immediately with the stir-fried greens and rice.

CANTONESE LEMON CHICKEN

SERVES 4

500 g (1 lb 2 oz) boneless, skinless
   chicken breasts

1 egg yolk, lightly beaten

2 teaspoons soy sauce

2 teaspoons dry sherry

3 teaspoons cornflour (cornstarch)

60 g (2¼ oz/½ cup) cornflour
   (cornstarch), extra

2½ tablespoons plain (all-purpose) flour

oil, for deep-frying

4 spring onions (scallions), thinly sliced

LEMON SAUCE

80 ml (2½ fl oz/⅓ cup) lemon juice

2 tablespoons sugar

1 tablespoon dry sherry

2 teaspoons cornflour (cornstarch)

1 **Cut the chicken** into long strips, about 1 cm (½ inch) wide, and then set aside. Combine the egg, 1 tablespoon water, soy sauce, sherry and cornflour in a small bowl and mix until smooth. Pour the egg mixture over the chicken, mixing well, and set aside for 10 minutes.

2 **Sift the extra cornflour** and plain flour together onto a plate. Roll each piece of chicken in the flour, coating each piece evenly, and shake off the excess. Place the chicken in a single layer on a plate.

3 **Fill a wok** one-third full of oil and heat to 180°C (350°F), or until a cube of bread dropped in the oil browns in 15 seconds. Carefully lower the chicken into the oil, in batches, and cook for 2 minutes, or until golden brown. Remove with a slotted spoon and drain on paper towel. Repeat with the remaining chicken. Set aside. Reserve the oil in the wok.

4 **To make the lemon sauce,** combine 2 tablespoons water, the lemon juice, sugar and sherry in a small saucepan. Bring to the boil over medium heat, stirring until the sugar dissolves. Stir the cornflour into 1 tablespoon water and mix to a smooth paste, then add to the lemon juice mixture, stirring constantly until the sauce boils and thickens. Set aside.

5 **Just before serving,** reheat the oil in the wok to very hot, add all the chicken pieces and deep-fry for 2 minutes, or until very crisp and a rich golden brown. Remove the chicken with a slotted spoon and drain well on paper towel. Pile chicken onto a serving plate, drizzle with the sauce and sprinkle with spring onion. Serve immediately.

Note: The first deep-frying of the chicken pieces can be done several hours in advance.

CARAMEL PORK AND PUMPKIN STIR-FRY

SERVES 4

250 g (9 oz/1¼ cups) jasmine rice

500 g (1 lb 2 oz) pork fillet, thinly sliced

2 garlic cloves, crushed

2–3 tablespoons peanut oil

300 g (11 oz) butternut pumpkin, cut into 2 cm (¾ inch) x 4 cm (1½ inch) pieces about 5 mm thick

60 g (2 oz/⅓ cup) soft brown sugar

60 ml (2 fl oz/¼ cup) fish sauce

60 ml (2 fl oz/¼ cup) rice vinegar

2 tablespoons chopped fresh coriander (cilantro) leaves

1.25 kg (2 lb 12 oz) mixed Asian greens (bok choy, choy sum, gai lam)

1 Bring a large saucepan of water to the boil. Add the rice and cook for 12 minutes, stirring occasionally. Drain.

2 Meanwhile, combine pork with garlic and 2 teaspoons of the peanut oil. Season with salt and plenty of pepper.

3 Heat a wok until very hot, add 1 tablespoon oil and swirl to coat. When just starting to smoke, stir-fry pork in two batches for about 1 minute per batch, or until the meat changes colour. Transfer to a plate. Add the remaining oil to the wok and stir-fry the pumpkin for 4 minutes, or until tender but not falling apart. Remove and add to the pork.

4 Combine the sugar, fish sauce, rice vinegar and 125 ml (4 fl oz/½ cup) water in the wok and boil for about 10 minutes, or until syrupy. Return the pork and pumpkin to the wok and stir for 1 minute, or until well coated and heated through. Stir in the coriander.

5 Put the mixed Asian greens in a paper-lined bamboo steamer over a wok of simmering water for 3 minutes, or until wilted. Serve immediately with the stir-fry and rice.

TORTILLA PIE

SERVES 4

1 tablespoon oil

500 g (1 lb. 2 oz) lean minced (ground) beef

35 g (1 oz) packet taco seasoning mix

420 g (14 oz) Mexican chilli beans, drained

8 flour tortillas

250 g (9 oz/2 cups) grated cheddar cheese

300 g (11 oz) Mexican tomato salsa

150 g (6 oz) sour cream

1 avocado, diced

1 Preheat oven to 180°C (350°F/Gas 4). Grease a 23 cm (9 inch) pie dish. Heat the oil in a large non-stick frying pan. Add the minced beef and cook for 5 minutes, or until brown, breaking up the lumps with the back of a spoon. Drain off the excess oil. Add the seasoning mix and cook for 5 minutes. Stir in the beans until heated through.

2 Lay a tortilla in the base of the pie dish, then spread 125 g (5 oz/½ cup) of the mince mixture on top. Sprinkle with 30 g (1 oz/¼ cup) cheese and 1 tablespoon salsa. Continue layering with the remaining tortillas, mince mixture, cheese and salsa, ending with a tortilla sprinkled with a little cheese—it should end up looking like a dome shape.

3 Bake for 15 minutes, or until all the cheese has melted and browned. Cool slightly, cut into wedges and top with a dollop of sour cream and the diced avocado. Serve with a tomato salad, if desired.

FILLET STEAK WITH MIXED MUSHROOMS AND SHERRY

250 g (9 oz) broccoli, cut into large florets

250 g (9 oz) green beans, topped and tailed

1 tablespoon oil

60 g (2 oz) butter

4 rib eye steaks (scotch fillet) about 160 g (6 oz) each, 2.5 cm (1 inch) thick

3 garlic cloves, finely chopped

250 g (9 oz) mixed mushrooms (portabello, Swiss brown, shiitake or button)

2 teaspoons chopped fresh thyme

125 ml (4 fl oz/½ cup) dry sherry

1 **Bring a saucepan** of lightly salted water to the boil. Add the broccoli and beans and cook for 3–4 minutes, or until tender but still crisp. Drain.

2 **Melt the oil** and 20 g (1 oz) of the butter in a large stainless steel frying pan. Cook the steaks for 3–4 minutes on each side for medium–rare, or until cooked to your liking. Remove from the pan, cover with foil and rest.

3 **Melt another 20 g (1 oz)** of the butter in the pan over medium heat. Add garlic and mushrooms and season to taste. Cook for 3–4 minutes, or until the mushrooms have softened. Stir in the thyme. Remove from the pan.

4 **Add the sherry** and any juices from the rested meat to the pan and stir to scrape up any sediment from the base. Bring to the boil, then reduce the heat and simmer for 2–3 minutes, or until reduced to about 4 tablespoons and thickened slightly. Whisk in the remaining butter in small amounts, until glossy.

5 **To serve,** put the steaks on four serving plates, top with the mushrooms and spoon the sauce over the top. Serve with the broccoli and green beans.

FISH & SEAFOOD

TUNA MORNAY

SERVES 4

60 g (2¼ oz) butter

2 tablespoons plain (all-purpose) flour

500 ml (17 fl oz/2 cups) milk

½ teaspoon dry mustard

90 g (3 oz/¾ cup) grated cheddar cheese

600 g (1 lb 5 oz) tinned tuna in brine, drained

2 tablespoons finely chopped parsley

2 eggs, hard-boiled and chopped

4 tablespoons fresh breadcrumbs

paprika, for dusting

1   Preheat the oven to 180°C (350°F/Gas 4). Melt butter in a small saucepan, add flour and stir over low heat for 1 minute. Take the pan off the heat and slowly pour in the milk, stirring with your other hand until you have a smooth sauce. Return the pan to the heat and stir constantly until the sauce boils and thickens. Reduce the heat and simmer for another 2 minutes. Remove the pan from the heat, whisk in the mustard and two-thirds of the cheese — don't stop whisking until you have a smooth, rich cheesy sauce.

2   Roughly flake the tuna with a fork, then tip it into the cheesy sauce, along with the parsley and egg. Season with a little salt and pepper. Spoon mixture into four 250 ml (9 fl oz/ 1 cup) ovenproof ramekins.

3   Make the topping by combining the breadcrumbs and the rest of the cheese, then sprinkle it over the mornay. Add a hint of colour by dusting the top very lightly with paprika. Place in the oven until the topping is golden brown, about 20 minutes.

BASIC PAN-FRIED FISH

SERVES 4

2–3 tablespoons plain (all-purpose) flour

4 blue-eye fish cutlets or jewfish, warehou, snapper or other firm white fish

olive oil, for shallow-frying

1 **Sift the flour** together with a little salt and freshly ground black pepper onto a plate. Pat the fish dry with paper towels, then coat both sides of the cutlets with seasoned flour, shaking off any excess.

2 **Heat about 3 mm** (⅝ inch) oil in a large frying pan until very hot. Put the fish into the hot oil and cook for 3 minutes on one side, then turn and cook the other side for 2 minutes, or until the coating is crisp and well browned. Reduce the heat to low and cook for another 2–3 minutes, or until the flesh flakes easily when tested with a fork.

3 **Remove fish** from the pan and drain briefly on crumpled paper towels. If you are cooking in batches, keep warm while cooking the remaining cutlets. Serve immediately with a green salad or some steamed vegetables.

BARBECUED SQUID WITH SALSA VERDE

SERVES 4

4 cleaned squid tubes

3 tablespoons olive oil

3 garlic cloves, crushed

150 g (6 oz) mixed lettuce leaves

250 g (9 oz/1 punnet) cherry tomatoes, halved

SALSA VERDE

2 large handfuls flat-leaf (Italian) parsley

2 tablespoons chopped dill

2 tablespoons extra virgin olive oil

2 tablespoons olive oil

1 tablespoon dijon mustard

2 garlic cloves, crushed

1 tablespoon red wine vinegar

1 tablespoon baby capers, rinsed and drained

4 anchovy fillets, drained

1 **Open the squid tubes** by cutting through one side so you have one large piece, the inside facing upwards. Pat dry with paper towels. Using a sharp knife, and being careful not to cut all the way through, score the flesh on the diagonal in a series of lines about 5 mm (¼ inch) apart, then do the same in the opposite direction to form a crisscross pattern. Cut squid into 4 cm (1½ inch) pieces and put in a non-metallic bowl.

2 **Combine oil** and garlic and pour over the squid, tossing to coat well. Cover and marinate in refrigerator for 30 minutes.

3 **Put all the salsa verde** ingredients in a food processor and blend until just combined. Set aside until ready to use.

4 **Preheat a barbecue** flat plate to high. Drain the squid and cook for 1–2 minutes, or until curled up and just cooked through. Put the squid in a bowl with the salsa verde and toss until well coated. Arrange the lettuce and tomatoes on four serving plates, top with squid, then season and serve.

SWORDFISH WITH TOMATO SALSA AND GARLIC MASH

SERVES 4

500 g (1 lb 2 oz) potatoes, cubed
2 large vine-ripened tomatoes
2 tablespoons finely shredded fresh basil
1 tablespoon balsamic vinegar
3 garlic cloves, finely chopped
145 ml (5 fl oz) olive oil
4 swordfish steaks (about 200 g/7 oz each)

1 **Cook the potato** in a large saucepan of boiling water for 12–15 minutes, or until tender.

2 **To make salsa,** score a cross in the base of each tomato. Place in a heatproof bowl and cover with boiling water. Leave for 30 seconds, then plunge into iced water and peel away from the cross. Cut the tomatoes in half, scoop out the seeds and discard. Finely dice the flesh, then combine with the basil, vinegar, 2 garlic cloves and 2 tablespoons oil. Season.

3 **Heat 3 tablespoons** of the olive oil in a large non-stick frying pan over medium–high heat. Season the swordfish well, then add to the frying pan and cook for 2–3 minutes on each side for medium–rare, or until cooked to your liking.

4 **Just before the swordfish** is ready, drain the potato. Add the remaining olive oil and garlic, and season to taste with salt and pepper. Mash until smooth with a potato masher.

5 **To serve,** put the swordfish steaks on four serving plates and top with the tomato salsa. Serve garlic mash on the side.

PRAWNS WITH GARLIC AND CHILLI

SERVES 4

125 ml (4 fl oz/½ cup) olive oil

6 garlic cloves, crushed

1 red onion, finely chopped

3–4 dried chillies, cut in half, seeds removed

1.125 kg (2 lb 7 oz/about 32) large prawns (shrimp), peeled

4 tomatoes, finely chopped

a handful parsley or coriander (cilantro), chopped

1 Heat the oil in a large frying pan or shallow casserole. Add the garlic, onion and chilli, cook for a few minutes until softened, then add the prawns and cook them for about 4 minutes, by which time they should be pink all over.

2 When the prawns are cooked, add the tomato and cook for a minute or two just to heat through. Season with salt and stir the herbs through.

3 Take the pan to the table straight away (the prawns will continue cooking in the heat), remembering to put it on a heatproof mat. Eat with bread to mop up the juices.

SHELLFISH STEW

SERVES 6

16 mussels
12 large prawns (shrimp)
435 ml (15 fl oz/1¾ cups) cider or dry white wine
50 g (2 oz) butter
1 garlic clove, crushed
2 shallots, finely chopped
2 celery stalks, finely chopped
1 large leek, white part only, thinly sliced
250 g (9 oz) small chestnut mushrooms, sliced
1 bay leaf
300 g (11 oz) salmon fillet, skinned and cut into chunks
400 g (14 oz) sole fillet, skinned and cut into thick strips widthways
300 ml (10½ fl oz) thick (double/heavy) cream
3 tablespoons finely chopped parsley

1   Scrub the mussels and remove their beards. Throw away any that are open and don't close when tapped on the bench. Peel and devein the prawns.

2   Pour cider into a large saucepan and bring to a simmer. Add mussels, cover the pan and cook for 3–5 minutes, shaking the pan every now and then. Place a fine sieve over a bowl, tip in the mussels, then transfer them to a plate; throw away any that haven't opened. Strain the cooking liquid again through the sieve.

3   Add the butter to the cleaned saucepan and melt over moderate heat. Add garlic, shallot, celery and leek and cook for 7–10 minutes, or until the vegetables are just soft. Add the mushrooms and cook for a further 4–5 minutes until softened. While the vegetables are cooking, remove the mussels from their shells.

4   Add the strained liquid to the vegetables in the saucepan, add the bay leaf and bring to a simmer. Add the salmon, sole and prawns and cook for 3–4 minutes until the fish is opaque and the prawns are pink. Stir in the cream and cooked mussels and simmer for 2 minutes. Season and stir in the parsley.

SALT AND PEPPER SQUID

SERVES 4

500 g (1 lb 2 oz) cleaned squid tubes

2 tablespoons lemon juice

2 garlic cloves, finely chopped

95 g (3 oz/½ cup) potato flour

1 tablespoon sichuan peppercorns, toasted and ground

1 tablespoon ground black pepper

1½ teaspoons ground white pepper

1½ tablespoons sea salt flakes, crushed

1 teaspoon caster (superfine) sugar

peanut oil, for deep-frying

lemon wedges, to serve

1 **Cut squid tubes** in half lengthways then lay them flat on the bench with the inside facing up. Score a shallow criss-cross pattern over this side only. Then cut into 5 x 3 cm (2 x 1¼ inch) rectangles.

2 **Combine the lemon juice** and garlic, then add the squid and toss to coat. Ideally, refrigerate for 1 hour, then drain off the marinade and discard. Combine the potato flour, peppers, salt and sugar and set aside.

3 **Fill a deep-fryer** or large heavy-based saucepan one-third full with the oil and heat to 180°C (350°F), or until a cube of bread dropped in the oil browns in 15 seconds.

4 **Coat the squid** in the flour mixture, pressing lightly into it to help it adhere.

5 **Deep-fry the squid** pieces in batches for 1½–2 minutes, or until lightly golden and curled. Drain well on paper towel and serve with lemon wedges.

SALMON AND POTATO PATTIES WITH MAYONNAISE

SERVES 4

400 g (14 oz) new potatoes, cut in half

2 teaspoons grated lime zest

310 g (11 oz/1¼ cups) whole-egg mayonnaise

425 g (15 oz) tinned salmon, drained, boned

1 tablespoon chopped fresh dill

2 spring onions (scallions), thinly sliced

1 egg

80 g (3 oz/1 cup) fresh breadcrumbs

3 tablespoons oil

200 g (7 oz) rocket (arugula) leaves

lime wedges, to serve

1 **Cook the potatoes** in a large saucepan of boiling water for 12–15 minutes, or until tender. Drain well and cool.

2 **Meanwhile,** combine the lime zest and 250 g (9 oz/1 cup) of the mayonnaise.

3 **Transfer the potato** to a large bowl, then mash roughly with the back of a spoon, leaving some large chunks. Stir in the salmon, dill and spring onion and season. Mix in the egg and the remaining mayonnaise. Divide into eight portions, forming palm-size patties. Press lightly into the breadcrumbs to coat.

4 **Heat the oil** in a non-stick frying pan and cook the patties, turning, for 3–4 minutes, or until golden brown. Drain on paper towels. Serve with a dollop of lime mayonnaise, rocket leaves and lime wedges.

TUNA STEAKS WITH OLIVE MAYONNAISE

SERVES 4

345 ml (12 fl oz) olive oil

2 egg yolks, at room temperature

25 ml (1 fl oz) lemon juice

40 g (1½ oz/⅓ cup) pitted black olives, chopped

200 g (7 oz) baby rocket (arugula) leaves

1 tablespoon finely chopped fresh rosemary

4 tuna steaks (about 200 g/7 oz each)

ready-made potato wedges, to serve (optional)

1 Process the egg yolks in a food processor, adding 3 tablespoons of the oil drop by drop. With the motor running, pour in 185 ml (6 fl oz/¾ cup) of the oil in a thin, steady stream until the mixture thickens and becomes creamy. With the motor still running, add 1 teaspoon of the lemon juice, season with salt and blend for 30 seconds. Transfer to a bowl, stir in the olives, cover and refrigerate.

2 To make the salad, toss the rocket leaves, 2 tablespoons oil and 1 tablespoon lemon juice in a bowl.

3 Press the rosemary into the tuna steaks. Heat remaining tablespoon of oil in a large frying pan and sear the tuna steaks over medium–high heat for 2–3 minutes on each side, or until cooked to your liking. Serve with a dollop of olive mayonnaise, some potato wedges and rocket salad.

Note: To save time, use 250 g (9 oz/1 cup) of good-quality whole-egg mayonnaise.

BLUE EYE CUTLETS IN A SPICY TOMATO SAUCE

SERVES 4

4 blue eye cutlets, 2.5 cm (1 inch) thick (about 250 g/9 oz each)

250 g (9 oz/1 cup) long-grain rice

2 tablespoons oil

1 teaspoon coriander seeds, lightly crushed

1 teaspoon black mustard seeds

1½ tablespoons sambal oelek

400 g (14 oz) tinned chopped tomatoes

1 teaspoon garam masala

300 g (10½ oz) baby English spinach leaves

1 **Preheat the oven** to 180°C (350°F/Gas 4). Pat the cutlets dry with paper towels. Bring a large saucepan of water to the boil. Add the rice and cook for 12 minutes, stirring occasionally. Drain well.

2 **Heat 1 tablespoon** of the oil in a saucepan over medium heat. When hot, add the coriander and mustard seeds — the seeds should start to pop after 30 seconds. Add the sambal oelek and cook for 30 seconds, then stir in the tomatoes and the garam masala. Bring to the boil, reduce the heat to low and simmer, covered, for 6–8 minutes, or until sauce thickens.

3 **Heat the remaining oil** in a large non-stick frying pan over medium heat. Add the cutlets and cook for 1 minute each side, or until evenly browned but not cooked through. Transfer to a large ceramic baking dish. Spoon tomato sauce over the cutlets and bake for 10 minutes, or until fish is cooked through.

4 **Meanwhile, wash the spinach** and put it in a saucepan with just the water clinging to the leaves. Cook, covered, for 1 minute, or until leaves have wilted. Serve the fish cutlets topped with sauce, with the spinach and the rice.

TERIYAKI SALMON FILLETS

SERVES 4

4 tablespoons soy sauce

4 tablespoons sake

4 tablespoons mirin

1 teaspoon sesame oil

2 tablespoons caster (superfine) sugar

2 teaspoon finely grated ginger

1 small garlic clove, crushed

4 x 200 g (7 oz) salmon fillets

oil spray

2 spring onions (scallions), chopped

1 Mix the soy sauce, sake, mirin, sesame oil, sugar, ginger and garlic together in a bowl. Put the fish in a shallow, non-metallic dish and pour the marinade over the top. Turn the fish in the marinade so it is well coated. Cover and marinate in the fridge for at least 3 hours.

2 Heat a large, heavy-based frying pan and spray with the oil. Lift the fish out of the marinade and drain. Cook the fish for 1–2 minutes, or until browned on each side, then cook at a lower heat for 3 minutes, or until fish is just cooked through.

3 Add the marinade and bring to a simmer, then remove the fish and simmer the sauce for 5 minutes, or until thick and sticky. Return the fish to the sauce to coat. Place the fish on a serving plate and pour over the sauce. Garnish with the spring onions and serve with rice.

Notes: Bottled teriyaki sauces are available from Asian food shops or supermarkets. Use Japanese soy sauce rather than Chinese soy sauce for a full-bodied flavour. Sake, mirin and sesame oil are available in supermarkets and Asian shops.

SWORDFISH WITH ANCHOVY AND CAPER SAUCE

SERVES 4

SAUCE

1 large garlic clove

1 tablespoon capers, rinsed and finely chopped

50 g (2 oz) anchovy fillets, finely chopped

1 tablespoon finely chopped rosemary or dried oregano

finely grated zest and juice of ½ lemon

4 tablespoons extra virgin olive oil

1 large tomato, finely chopped

4 swordfish steaks

1 tablespoon extra virgin olive oil

crusty Italian bread, to serve

1 Put the garlic in a mortar and pestle with a little salt and crush it. To make the sauce, mix together the garlic, capers, anchovies, rosemary or oregano, lemon zest and juice, oil and tomato. Leave for 10 minutes.

2 Preheat a griddle or grill (broiler) to very hot. Using paper towels, pat the swordfish dry and lightly brush with the olive oil. Season with salt and pepper. Sear the swordfish over high heat for about 2 minutes on each side (depending on the thickness of the steaks), or until just cooked. The best way to check if fish is cooked is to pull apart the centre of one steak — the flesh should be opaque. (Serve with cut side underneath.)

3 If the cooked swordfish is a little oily, drain it on paper towels, then place on serving plates and drizzle with the sauce. Serve with Italian bread to mop up the sauce.

INDIAN-STYLE BUTTER PRAWNS

SERVES 4

1 kg (2 lb 4 oz) large raw prawns
(shrimp)

100 g (4 oz) butter

2 large garlic cloves, crushed

1 teaspoon ground cumin

1 teaspoon paprika

1½ teaspoons garam masala

2 tablespoons good-quality ready-made
tandoori paste

2 tablespoons tomato paste
(concentrated purée)

300 ml (10½ fl oz) thick (double/heavy)
cream

1 teaspoon sugar

90 g (3 oz/⅓ cup) plain yoghurt

2 tablespoons chopped coriander
(cilantro) leaves

1 tablespoon flaked almonds, toasted

lemon wedges, to serve

1 **Peel and devein prawns,** leaving tails intact. Melt butter
in a large saucepan over medium heat, then add the garlic,
cumin, paprika and 1 teaspoon of garam masala and cook for
1 minute, or until fragrant. Add the tandoori paste and tomato
paste, and cook for a further 2 minutes. Stir in the cream and
sugar, then reduce the heat and simmer for 10 minutes, or
until the sauce thickens slightly.

2 **Add the prawns** to the pan and cook for 8–10 minutes, or
until they are pink and cooked through. Remove the pan from
the heat and stir in the yoghurt, the remaining garam masala
and half the coriander. Season.

3 **Garnish with** the flaked almonds and remaining coriander
and serve with steamed rice and lemon wedges.

Note: This dish is very rich so we recommend that you serve
it with steamed vegetables or a fresh salad.

GARLIC AND GINGER PRAWNS

1 kg (2 lb 4 oz) large raw prawns (shrimp)

2 tablespoons oil

3–4 garlic cloves, finely chopped

5 cm (2 inch) piece fresh ginger, cut into matchsticks

2–3 small red chillies, seeded and finely chopped

6 coriander (cilantro) roots, finely chopped, plus a few leaves to garnish

8 spring onions (scallions), cut into short lengths

½ red capsicum (pepper), thinly sliced

2 tablespoons lemon juice

125 ml (4 fl oz/½ cup) white wine

1 teaspoon crushed palm sugar (jaggery) or soft brown sugar

2 teaspoons fish sauce

1 **Peel the prawns,** leaving the tails intact. Gently cut a slit down the back of each prawn and remove the dark vein.

2 **Heat a wok** until very hot, add the oil and swirl it around to coat the side. Stir-fry half of the prawns, garlic, ginger, chilli and coriander root for 1–2 minutes over high heat, or until prawns have just turned pink. Remove from the wok. Repeat with the remaining prawns, garlic, ginger, chilli and coriander root. Remove all the prawns from the wok; set aside.

3 **Add the spring onion** and pepper to the wok. Cook over high heat for 2–3 minutes. Add the combined lemon juice, wine and palm sugar. Boil until liquid is reduced by two thirds.

4 **Return the prawns** to the wok and sprinkle with the fish sauce, to taste. Toss until the prawns are heated through. Remove from the heat and sprinkle with coriander leaves.

STEAMED WHOLE FISH WITH CHILLI, GARLIC AND LIME

SERVES 4–6

1–1.5 kg (2 lb 4 oz–3 lb 5 oz) whole
   snapper

1 lime, sliced

red chillies, finely chopped, to garnish

coriander (cilantro) leaves, to garnish

lime wedges, to garnish

SAUCE

2 teaspoons tamarind concentrate

5 long red chillies, seeded and chopped

6 large garlic cloves, roughly chopped

6 coriander (cilantro) roots and stalks

8 red Asian shallots, chopped

1½ tablespoons oil

2½ tablespoons lime juice

130 g (4½ oz/¾ cup) shaved palm sugar
   (jaggery) or soft brown sugar

3 tablespoons fish sauce

1   **Rinse the fish** and pat dry with paper towels. Cut two diagonal slashes through the thickest part of the fish on both sides, to ensure even cooking. Place the lime slices in the fish cavity, cover with plastic wrap and chill until ready to use.

2   **To make the sauce,** combine tamarind with 3 tablespoons water. Blend the chilli, garlic, coriander and shallots in a food processor until finely puréed — add a little water, if needed.

3   **Heat the oil** in a saucepan. Add the paste and cook over medium heat for 5 minutes, or until fragrant. Stir in the tamarind, lime juice and palm sugar. Reduce the heat and simmer for 10 minutes, or until thick. Add the fish sauce.

4   **Place the fish** on a sheet of baking paper in a large bamboo steamer and cover. Place over a wok of simmering water — ensure the base doesn't touch the water. Cook for 6 minutes per 1 kg (2 lb 4 oz) fish, or until flesh flakes easily with a fork.

5   **Pour the sauce** over the fish and garnish with the chilli, coriander and lime wedges. Serve with rice.

FRESH TUNA AND GREEN BEAN STIR-FRY

SERVES 4

300 g (11 oz) small green beans, trimmed

2 tablespoons oil

600 g (1 lb 5 oz) piece of tuna, cut into small cubes

250 g (9 oz/1½ cups) small cherry tomatoes

16 small black olives

2–3 tablespoons lemon juice

2 garlic cloves, finely chopped

8 anchovy fillets, rinsed, dried and finely chopped

3 tablespoons small basil leaves

1 Blanch the beans in a small saucepan of boiling water for 2 minutes. Drain and refresh under cold water to arrest the cooking, then set aside.

2 Heat a wok until very hot, add the oil and swirl it around to coat the side. Stir-fry tuna in batches for about 5 minutes each batch, or until cooked on the outside but still a little pink on the inside. If necessary, heat a little more oil for each batch.

3 Add the cherry tomatoes, olives and beans to the wok, then gently toss for a minute or so until heated through. Add the lemon juice, garlic and anchovies and stir well. Season to taste with salt and freshly ground black pepper. Serve scattered with the basil leaves.

CRUNCHY FISH FILLETS WITH CHIVE MAYO

SERVES 4

160 g (6 oz/⅔ cup) good-quality ready
    made mayonnaise

2 tablespoons snipped chives

1 tablespoon sweet chilli sauce

75 g (3 oz/½ cup) cornmeal

4 x 200 g (7 oz) skinless perch fillets

3 tablespoons oil

1 For the chive mayo, combine the mayonnaise, chives and chilli sauce in a small bowl. Keep refrigerated until needed.

2 Put the cornmeal on a plate. Score four diagonal slashes in the skin side of each fish fillet, to prevent the fish curling during cooking. Press both sides of the fillets into the cornmeal to coat thoroughly.

3 Heat the oil in a frying pan over medium heat. Add fish and cook for 3 minutes. Turn and cook for another 3 minutes, or until tender and the fish flakes easily. Remove and drain. Serve with the chive mayo.

BEER-BATTERED FISH FILLETS WITH CHIPS

SERVES 4

30 g (1 oz/¼ cup) self-raising flour

30 g (1 oz/¼ cup) cornflour (cornstarch)

125 g (5 oz/1 cup) plain (all-purpose) flour

250 ml (9 fl oz/1 cup) beer (use any type to vary the flavour)

oil, for deep-frying

4 large pontiac potatoes, cut into finger-size chips

4 flathead fillets (about 200 g/7 oz each), or other white fish fillets (snapper, blue eye or John Dory), skinned

2 lemons, cut into wedges

1 Preheat the oven to 180°C (350°F/Gas 4). Sift self-raising flour, cornflour and 60 g (2 oz/½ cup) of the plain flour into a large bowl and make a well. Gradually whisk in the beer to make a smooth batter. Cover.

2 Fill a large heavy-based saucepan one-third full of oil and heat to 180°C (350°F), or until a cube of bread dropped into the oil browns in 15 seconds. Deep-fry batches of potato chips for 2–4 minutes, or until pale golden. Drain on paper towels. Deep-fry again for 3 minutes, or until golden and cooked through. Keep hot in oven while you cook the fish.

3 Reheat the oil to 180°C (350°F). Stir the batter, then coat the fish fillets in the remaining plain flour, shaking off the excess. Dip the fillets into the batter, allowing the excess to drip off a little. Slowly ease the fillets into the hot oil, holding the tail out for a few seconds — turn with tongs if necessary. Cook for 4–5 minutes, or until golden brown and the fish is cooked through. Remove with a slotted spoon and drain on crumpled paper towels. Serve with the chips, lemon wedges and a green salad.

TUNA WITH LIME AND CHILLI SAUCE

SERVES 4

SAUCE

2 large handfuls mint, chopped

2 large handfuls coriander (cilantro) leaves, chopped

1 teaspoon grated lime zest

1 tablespoon lime juice

1 teaspoon grated fresh ginger

1 jalapeno chilli, seeded and finely chopped (see Note)

250 g (9 oz/1 cup) low-fat plain yoghurt

canola oil spray

4 tuna steaks

175 g (6 oz) asparagus, trimmed and cut into 5 cm (2 inch) pieces

125 g (5 oz) snowpeas (mangetout), trimmed

125 g (5 oz) green beans, trimmed

4 wholegrain bread rolls, to serve

1   To make the sauce, combine mint, coriander, lime zest, lime juice, ginger and chilli. Fold in the yoghurt and season with salt and freshly ground black pepper.

2   Heat a chargrill pan over high heat and lightly spray with the oil. Cook the tuna steaks for 2 minutes on each side, or until cooked, but still pink in the centre.

3   Meanwhile, steam the vegetables for 2–3 minutes, or until just tender.

4   Top the tuna with the sauce. Serve with the vegetables and bread.

Note: Jalapeno chillies are smooth and thick-fleshed and are available both red and green. They are quite fiery, so you can use a less powerful variety of chilli if you prefer.

TUNA BURGERS WITH HERBED MAYONNAISE

SERVES 4

4 garlic cloves, crushed

2 egg yolks

250 ml (9 fl oz/1 cup) light olive oil

3 tablespoons chopped flat-leaf (Italian) parsley

1 tablespoon chopped dill

2 teaspoons dijon mustard

1 tablespoon lemon juice

1 tablespoon red wine vinegar

1 tablespoon baby capers in brine, drained

4 anchovy fillets in oil, drained

4 x 150 g (6 oz) tuna steaks

2 tablespoons olive oil

2 red onions, thinly sliced

4 large round bread rolls, halved and buttered

100 g (4 oz) mixed lettuce leaves

1 **Put garlic and egg yolks** in a food processor and process for 10 seconds. With the motor running, add oil in a very thin, slow stream. When the mixture starts to thicken, start pouring the oil a little faster until all it has been added and the mixture is thick and creamy. Add the parsley, dill, mustard, lemon juice, vinegar, capers and anchovies, and process until the mixture is smooth. Refrigerate the mayonnaise until needed.

2 **Preheat the chargrill** plate to high direct heat. Brush tuna steaks with 1 tablespoon of olive oil and cook for 2 minutes on each side, or until they are almost cooked through. Add the remaining olive oil to the onion, toss to separate and coat the rings, and cook on the flat plate for 2 minutes, or until the onion is soft and caramelized. Toast the rolls, buttered-side down, on the chargrill plate for 1 minute, or until they are marked and golden.

3 **Put some lettuce,** a tuna steak, some of the onion and a dollop of herbed mayonnaise on one half of each roll. Season and top with the other half of the roll.

THAI PRAWN CURRY

SERVES 4

CURRY PASTE

1 small onion, roughly chopped

3 garlic cloves

4 dried red chillies

4 whole black peppercorns

2 tablespoons chopped lemongrass, white part only

1 tablespoon chopped coriander (cilantro) root

2 teaspoons grated lime zest

2 teaspoons cumin seeds

1 teaspoon sweet paprika

1 teaspoon ground coriander

2 tablespoons oil

1 tablespoon oil

2 tablespoons fish sauce

2 cm (¾ inch) piece of fresh galangal, thinly sliced

4 makrut (kaffir lime) leaves

400 ml (14 fl oz) tinned coconut cream

1 kg (2 lb 4 oz) prawns (shrimp), peeled and deveined, tails intact

sliced fresh red chillies, to garnish (optional)

coriander (cilantro) leaves, to garnish

1 To make the curry paste, put all the ingredients and 1 teaspoon salt in a small food processor. Process until the mixture forms a smooth paste.

2 Heat the oil in a pan. Add half the curry paste and stir over low heat for 30 seconds. Add the fish sauce, galangal, lime leaves and coconut cream, and stir until combined.

3 Add the prawns to the pan and simmer, uncovered, for 10 minutes, or until the prawns are cooked and sauce has thickened slightly. Sprinkle with chilli and coriander leaves. Serve with steamed rice.

CATALAN FISH STEW

SERVES 6–8

CATALAN FISH STEW

300 g (11 oz) red mullet fillets

400 g (14 oz) firm white fish fillets

300 g (11 oz) cleaned calamari

1.5 litres (52 fl oz/6 cups) fish stock

4 tablespoons olive oil

1 onion, chopped

6 garlic cloves, chopped

1 small fresh red chilli, chopped

1 teaspoon paprika

pinch saffron threads

150 ml (5 fl oz) white wine

425 g (15 oz) tinned chopped tomatoes

16 raw prawns (shrimp), peeled, tails intact

2 tablespoons brandy

24 black mussels, cleaned

1 tablespoon chopped fresh parsley, to garnish

PICADA

2 tablespoons olive oil

2 slices day-old bread, cubed

2 garlic cloves

5 blanched almonds, toasted

2 tablespoons fresh flat-leaf (Italian) parsley

1 Cut the fish and calamari into small pieces. Place stock in a large saucepan and bring to the boil for 15 minutes, or until liquid has reduced a little.

2 To make the picada, heat the oil in a frying pan and cook the bread, stirring, for 2 minutes, or until golden, adding the garlic for the last minute. Place all of the ingredients in a food processor and process, gradually adding stock to make a smooth but not too runny paste.

3 Heat 2 tablespoons of the oil in a saucepan, add the onion, garlic, chilli and paprika, and cook, stirring, for 1 minute. Add the saffron, wine, tomatoes and stock. Bring to the boil, then reduce the heat and simmer. Heat the remaining oil in a frying pan and fry the fish and the calamari for 3–5 minutes. Remove from the pan. Add the prawns, cook for 1 minute, then pour in the brandy. Carefully ignite the brandy and let the flames burn down. Remove prawns from the pan.

4 Add mussels to the pan and simmer, covered, for about 3 minutes, or until opened. Discard any that do not open. Add all the seafood and the picada to the pan, stirring until sauce has thickened. Season, sprinkle with the parsley and serve.

VEGETARIAN

TOFU BURGERS

SERVES 6

olive oil, for pan-frying

1 red onion, finely chopped

200 g (7 oz) Swiss brown mushrooms, finely chopped

350 g (12 oz) hard tofu

2 large garlic cloves, peeled

3 tablespoons chopped basil

200 g (7 oz/2 cups) dry wholemeal (whole-wheat) breadcrumbs, plus 150 g (5½ oz/1½ cups), for coating

1 egg, lightly beaten

2 tablespoons balsamic vinegar

2 tablespoons sweet chilli sauce, plus extra, to serve

6 bread rolls

ready-made mayonnaise, to serve

100 g (4 oz/⅔ cup) semi-dried (sun-blushed) tomatoes

a large handful of rocket (arugula) leaves

1   Heat **1 tablespoon** of olive oil in a frying pan. Sauté the onion over medium heat for 5 minutes, or until soft. Add the mushrooms and cook for a further 2 minutes, then leave to cool slightly.

2   Put **250 g (9 oz)** of the tofu in a food processor with the garlic and basil and blend until smooth. Tip into a large bowl and stir in the onion mixture, breadcrumbs, egg, vinegar and sweet chilli sauce. Grate the remaining tofu and fold it through the mixture, then refrigerate for 30 minutes.

3   Divide the tofu mixture into six even portions and form into patties, pressing together firmly. Then coat them in the extra breadcrumbs.

4   Heat **1 cm (½ inch)** oil in a deep frying pan. Cook the patties in two batches for 4–5 minutes on each side, or until golden (turn them carefully so they don't break up). Drain on paper towels and season with sea salt.

5   Cut the bread rolls in half and toast under a hot grill (broiler). Spread with mayonnaise, then layer with the tomatoes, a tofu patty and rocket. Drizzle with sweet chilli sauce, top with the burger lid and serve.

STUFFED MUSHROOMS WITH SPICED COUSCOUS

MAKES 8

8 field mushrooms

95 g (3 oz/½ cup) instant couscous

1 tablespoon extra virgin olive oil

1 teaspoon ground cumin

¼ teaspoon cayenne pepper

2 teaspoons finely grated lemon zest

125 ml (4 fl oz/½ cup) vegetable stock
or water

1 tomato, finely chopped

1 tablespoon lemon juice

2 tablespoons chopped fresh flat-leaf
(Italian) parsley

2 tablespoons chopped fresh mint

1 **Peel the mushrooms** and remove the stalks, then grill them top-side up.

2 **Meanwhile, place couscous,** olive oil, cumin, cayenne pepper and lemon zest in a bowl. Season, then stir flavourings through the couscous.

3 **Bring the chicken stock** to the boil and stir it into the couscous. Cover and leave for 5 minutes, then fluff the grains with a fork. Stir in the tomato, lemon juice, parsley and mint. Fill each mushroom cap with some of the couscous mixture and pack down firmly. Grill until the couscous is golden. Serve hot or cold.

CREAMY ZUCCHINI OMELETTE

SERVES 2

2 zucchini (courgettes)

2 tablespoons olive oil

60 g (2 oz) butter

1 garlic clove, finely chopped

5 eggs

2 tablespoons pouring cream

2 tablespoons grated parmesan cheese

1   **Trim the zucchini** and cut lengthways into very thin slices.

2   **Heat half the olive oil** and half the butter in a frying pan until the butter melts. Add the zucchini and sauté over medium heat for 2–3 minutes, or until golden. Stir in the garlic and cook for a further 30 seconds. Using a slotted spoon, transfer the mixture to a plate. Wipe the pan clean.

3   **Crack eggs** into a bowl. Add the cream, season with sea salt and freshly ground black pepper and whisk to combine.

4   **Reheat the pan** and add the remaining oil and butter. When the pan is very hot, pour in the eggs and stir with the back of a fork. Cook for 1 minute, tilting the pan and lifting the omelette edges occasionally to allow the uncooked egg to run underneath.

5   **When the egg** is partly set, spread the zucchini mixture over the top. Reduce the heat and cook for 5 minutes, or until set around the edges. Remove from the heat and sprinkle with the parmesan. Cover with a lid and leave to rest in the pan for 2 minutes. Slide onto a plate, fold into a semi-circle, cut in half and serve.

VEGETABLE STACKS WITH SPICY TOMATO SAUCE

125 m (4 fl oz/1½ cup) oil

2 zucchini (courgettes), sliced on the diagonal

500 g (1 lb 2 oz) eggplant (aubergines), sliced

1 small fennel bulb, sliced

1 red onion, sliced

300 g (11 oz) ricotta cheese

50 g (2 oz/½ cup) grated parmesan cheese

1 tablespoon chopped flat-leaf (Italian) parsley

1 tablespoon snipped chives

1 red and 1 yellow capsicum (pepper), grilled (broiled), peeled, cut into large pieces

SPICY TOMATO SAUCE

1 tablespoon oil

1 onion, finely chopped

2 garlic cloves, crushed

1 red chilli, seeded and chopped

425 g (15 oz) tin chopped tomatoes

2 tablespoons tomato paste (purée)

1 **Heat 1 tablespoon of the oil** in a large frying pan over high heat. Cook the zucchini, eggplant, fennel and onion in batches for 5 minutes, or until golden, adding oil as needed. Drain separately on paper towels.

2 **Preheat the oven** to 200°C (400°F/ Gas 6). Combine the ricotta, parmesan, parsley and chives. Season well.

3 **Lightly grease** and line four 315 ml (11 fl oz/1¼ cup) ramekins. Use half the eggplant to line the base of each dish. Continue layering with the zucchini, capsicum, cheese mixture, fennel and onion. Cover with the remaining eggplant and press down firmly. Bake for 10–15 minutes, or until hot. Leave for 5 minutes before turning out.

4 **Meanwhile,** to make the sauce, heat the oil in a saucepan and cook the onion and garlic for 3 minutes, or until soft. Add the chilli, chopped tomato and tomato paste and simmer for 5 minutes, or until thick and pulpy. Purée in a food processor. Return to the pan and keep warm. Spoon over the terrines.

LENTIL AND CHICKPEA BURGERS WITH GARLIC CREAM

MAKES 10 BURGERS

1 tablespoon olive oil, plus extra,
  for pan-frying

2 onions, sliced

1 tablespoon tandoori mix powder

425 g (15 oz) tin chickpeas, drained
  and rinsed

1 tablespoon grated fresh ginger

1 egg

250 g (9 oz/1 cup) red lentils, cooked

3 tablespoons chopped parsley

2 tablespoons chopped coriander
  (cilantro)

180 g (6 oz/2 cups) dry breadcrumbs

flour, for dusting

CORIANDER GARLIC CREAM

125 g (5 oz/½ cup) sour cream

125 ml (4 fl oz/½ cup) pouring cream

1 garlic clove, crushed

2 tablespoons chopped coriander
  (cilantro)

2 tablespoons chopped parsley

1 Heat the olive oil in a frying pan. Sauté the onion over medium heat for 5 minutes, or until softened. Add the tandoori mix and stir until fragrant, then leave to cool slightly.

2 Put the onion in a food processor with the chickpeas, ginger, egg and half the lentils. Blend for 20 seconds, or until smooth. Transfer to a bowl, add the remaining lentils, parsley, coriander and breadcrumbs and mix well.

3 Divide into 10 portions and shape into patties. (If mixture is too soft, refrigerate for 15 minutes; the mixture can be made up to 2 days ahead.) Toss patties in flour; shake off the excess.

4 Heat a frying pan and brush lightly with oil. Add the patties in batches and cook over medium heat for 3–4 minutes on each side, or until browned. Keep warm.

5 Put all the coriander garlic cream ingredients in a bowl and mix well. Serve with the hot patties.

VEGETABLE LENTIL SOUP WITH SPICED YOGHURT

SERVES 6

2 tablespoons olive oil

1 small leek, white part only, chopped

2 garlic cloves, crushed

2 teaspoons curry powder

1 teaspoon ground cumin

1 teaspoon garam masala

1 litre (35 fl oz/4 cups) vegetable stock

1 bay leaf

185 g (7 oz/1 cup) brown lentils

450 g (1 lb) butternut pumpkin (squash), peeled and cut into 1 cm (½ inch) dice

2 zucchini (courgettes), cut in half lengthways and sliced

400 g (14 oz) tin chopped tomatoes

200 g (7 oz) broccoli, cut into small florets

1 small carrot, diced

80 g (3 oz/½ cup) fresh or frozen peas

1 tablespoon shredded mint

SPICED YOGHURT

250 g (9 oz/1 cup) Greek-style yoghurt

1 tablespoon chopped coriander (cilantro) leaves

1 garlic clove, crushed

3 dashes of Tabasco sauce

1 Heat the olive oil in a large heavy-based saucepan. Sauté the leek and garlic over medium heat for 5 minutes, or until lightly golden. Add the spices and cook for 1 minute, or until fragrant.

2 Add stock, bay leaf, lentils and pumpkin. Bring to the boil, then reduce the heat to low and simmer for 10–15 minutes, or until the lentils are tender. Season well.

3 Add the zucchini, tomato, broccoli, carrot and 500 ml (17 fl oz/2 cups) water and simmer for 10 minutes, or until vegetables are tender. Add peas and simmer for 2–3 minutes.

4 Meanwhile, put the spiced yoghurt ingredients in a small bowl and mix well.

5 Ladle the soup into bowls. Dollop with the yoghurt and serve sprinkled with mint.

GREEN CURRY WITH SWEET POTATO AND EGGPLANT

SERVES 4–6

1 tablespoon vegetable oil

1 onion, chopped

1–2 tablespoons green curry paste

1 eggplant (aubergine), quartered and sliced

400 ml (14 fl oz) tin coconut milk

250 ml (9 fl oz/1 cup) vegetable stock

6 makrut (kaffir lime) leaves, plus extra shredded makrut leaves, to serve

1 orange sweet potato, peeled and diced

2 teaspoons soft brown sugar

2 teaspoons lime zest

2 tablespoons lime juice

coriander (cilantro) leaves, to garnish

steamed jasmine rice, to serve

1 **Heat the oil** in a large wok or frying pan. Add onion and curry paste and cook, stirring, over medium heat for 3 minutes. Add eggplant and cook for 4–5 minutes, or until softened.

2 **Pour in the coconut milk** and stock. Bring to the boil, then reduce the heat and simmer for 5 minutes. Add the lime leaves and sweet potato and cook, stirring occasionally, for 10 minutes, or until the vegetables are very tender.

3 **Mix in the sugar**, lime zest and lime juice until well combined. Season to taste with sea salt. Serve garnished with coriander leaves and shredded lime leaves, with steamed jasmine rice.

PHAD THAI

SERVES 4

400 g (14 oz) dried flat rice stick noodles

2 tablespoons peanut oil

2 eggs, lightly beaten

1 onion, cut into thin wedges

2 garlic cloves, crushed

1 small red capsicum (pepper), cut into thin strips

100 g (4 oz) fried tofu, cut into strips 5 mm (¼ inch) wide

6 spring onions (scallions), thinly sliced on the diagonal

a handful of chopped coriander (cilantro) leaves

60 ml (2 fl oz/¼ cup) soy sauce

2 tablespoons lime juice

1 tablespoon soft brown sugar

2 teaspoons sambal oelek or chilli sauce

90 g (3 oz/1 cup) bean sprouts, tails trimmed

40 g (1½ oz/¼ cup) chopped roasted unsalted peanuts

1 Cook noodles in a pan of boiling water for 5–10 minutes, or until tender. Drain and set aside.

2 Heat a wok over high heat and swirl in enough peanut oil to coat the bottom and side. When the oil is smoking, add the egg and swirl to form a thin omelette. Cook for 30 seconds, or until just set. Roll up, remove from the pan and thinly slice.

3 Heat the remaining oil in the wok. Stir-fry the onion, garlic and capsicum over high heat for 2–3 minutes, or until the onion has softened. Add the noodles, tossing well. Stir in the omelette, tofu, spring onion and half the coriander.

4 Combine the soy sauce, lime juice, sugar and sambal oelek, then pour it over the noodles and toss to coat. Sprinkle the bean shoots over the top and garnish with the peanuts and the remaining coriander. Serve immediately.

TOFU WITH CHILLI RELISH AND CASHEWS

SERVES 4

CHILLI RELISH

80 ml (3 fl oz/⅓ cup) peanut oil

12 red Asian shallots, chopped

8 garlic cloves, chopped

8 long red chillies, chopped

2 red capsicums (peppers), chopped

1 tablespoon tamarind concentrate

1 tablespoon soy sauce

100 g (4 oz/¾ cup) grated palm sugar
(jaggery), or soft brown sugar

2 tablespoons kecap manis

1 tablespoon peanut oil

6 spring onions (scallions), cut into
3 cm (1¼ inch) lengths

750 g (1 lb 10 oz) silken firm tofu, cut
into 3 cm (1¼ inch) dice

a large handful of Thai basil

100 g (4 oz/⅔ cup) roasted salted
cashew nuts

steamed rice, to serve

1 **To make the chilli relish,** heat half the peanut oil in a frying pan and sauté the shallot and garlic over medium heat for 2 minutes. Transfer to a food processor, add the chilli and capsicum and process until smooth. Heat the remaining oil in the pan, add the shallot mixture and cook over medium heat for 2 minutes. Stir in the tamarind, soy sauce and sugar and cook for 20 minutes, stirring occasionally.

2 Put 2–3 tablespoons of the relish in a small bowl (store the remainder in a small airtight jar in the fridge). Add the kecap manis, mix well and set aside.

3 Heat a wok until very hot. Add the peanut oil and swirl to coat the side. Stir-fry the spring onion over medium–high heat for 30 seconds, then remove from the wok.

4 **Stir-fry the tofu** for 1 minute, then stir in relish mixture. Cook for 3 minutes, or until tofu is coated and heated through. Toss spring onion, Thai basil and cashews through and stir-fry just until the basil has wilted. Serve with steamed rice.

YELLOW CURRY WITH PUMPKIN AND GREEN BEANS

SERVES 4

500 ml (17 fl oz/2 cups) coconut cream

3 teaspoons yellow curry paste

125 ml (4 fl oz/½ cup) vegetable stock

500 g (1 lb 2 oz) jap or kent pumpkin (winter squash), peeled and diced

300 g (11 oz) green beans, trimmed and halved

2 tablespoons soy sauce

2 tablespoons lime juice

1 tablespoon grated palm sugar (jaggery) or soft brown sugar

3 tablespoons coriander (cilantro) leaves

40 g (1½ oz/¼ cup) cashew nuts, toasted

steamed jasmine rice, to serve

1 Without shaking the tin of coconut cream, spoon the thick cream from the top of the tin into a wok and heat until boiling. Add the curry paste, then reduce the heat and simmer, stirring, for 5 minutes, until the cream begins to separate.

2 Stir in remaining coconut cream, stock and pumpkin; simmer for 10 minutes. Add the beans and cook for a further 8 minutes, or until the vegetables are tender.

3 Gently stir in the soy sauce, lime juice and palm sugar until well combined. Serve scattered with the coriander leaves and cashews, with steamed jasmine rice.

TOMATO AND PASTA SOUP

SERVES 4

1.25 litres (45 fl oz/5 cups) vegetable stock

90 g (3 oz/1 cup) spiral pasta

2 carrots, sliced

1 zucchini (courgette), sliced

4 ripe tomatoes, roughly chopped

2 tablespoons shredded basil

fresh wholemeal loaf, to serve

1 **Place the stock** in a heavy-based saucepan and bring to the boil. Reduce the heat, add the pasta, carrot and zucchini and cook for about 5–10 minutes, or until the pasta is al dente.

2 **Add the tomato** and heat through gently for a few more minutes. Season to taste.

3 **Pour the soup** into warm soup bowls and sprinkle the basil over the top. Serve with a fresh wholemeal loaf.

Variation: To give this soup even more of a Mediterranean flavour, serve it with a dollop of pesto. Pesto is available in tubs and jars at the supermarket.

HUNGARIAN CASSEROLE

SERVES 4–6

1 tablespoon olive oil

30 g (1 oz) butter

4 large all-purpose potatoes, peeled and cut into large chunks

1 onion, chopped

1 red capsicum (pepper), roughly chopped

1 green capsicum (pepper), roughly chopped

440 g (14 oz) tin chopped tomatoes

250 ml (9 fl oz/1 cup) vegetable stock

2 teaspoons caraway seeds

2 teaspoons paprika

CROUTONS

4 thick slices of white bread

250 ml (9 fl oz/1 cup) vegetable oil

1 **Heat the olive oil** and butter in a large heavy-based saucepan. Add the potatoes and cook over medium heat, turning regularly, until crisp on the edges.

2 **Add the onion** and red and green capsicum and sauté for 5 minutes. Stir in the tomato, stock, caraway seeds and paprika and season to taste with sea salt and freshly ground black pepper. Simmer, uncovered, for 10 minutes, or until the potatoes are tender.

3 **Meanwhile,** make the croutons. Cut crusts off the bread and discard, then cut the bread into small cubes. Heat the oil in a frying pan over medium heat. Add the bread cubes and cook for 2 minutes, or until golden brown and crisp, turning often. Drain on paper towels, scatter over the casserole and serve immediately.

SPRING VEGETABLE SOUP WITH BASIL PESTO

SERVES 4

1.25 litres (45 fl oz/5 cups) vegetable
    stock

1 tablespoon extra virgin olive oil

8 spring onions (scallions), finely sliced

2 celery stalks, finely sliced

12 baby (dutch) carrots, sliced

310 g (11 oz/2 bunches) asparagus,
    woody ends removed, cut into 2.5 cm
    (1 inch) lengths

150 g (6 oz) baby corn, cut into 2.5 cm
    (1 inch) lengths

60 g (2 oz/¼ cup) fresh or bottled pesto

extra virgin olive oil, to thin pesto
    (see Note)

shaved parmesan cheese, to garnish

1 **Bring the stock** to the boil in a large saucepan. Meanwhile, heat the olive oil in a large heavy-based saucepan and add the spring onion and celery. Cover and cook over medium heat for 5 minutes, or until softened.

2 **Add the stock** to the spring onion mixture and mix well.

3 **Add the carrot,** asparagus and corn to the pan. Return the mixture to the boil, then reduce the heat and simmer for 10 minutes.

4 **Spoon into** warmed soup bowls.

5 **Top with a dollop of pesto,** season to taste with salt and pepper, and garnish with shaved parmesan.

Note: Home-made pesto or fresh pesto from a deli will give a better flavour than bottled pesto. If you prefer a thinner pesto, mix it with a little olive oil to give it a runnier consistency.

WARM CASARECCI AND SWEET POTATO SALAD

SERVES 4

750 g (1 lb 10 oz) orange sweet potato

2 tablespoons extra virgin olive oil

500 g (1 lb 2 oz) casarecci pasta

325 g (11 oz) marinated feta cheese in oil

3 tablespoons balsamic vinegar

155 g (1 bunch) asparagus, cut into short lengths

100 g (4 oz) baby rocket (arugula) or baby English spinach leaves

2 vine-ripened tomatoes, chopped

40 g (1½ oz/¼ cup) pine nuts, toasted

1 **Preheat the oven** to 200°C (400°F/Gas 6). Peel the sweet potato and cut into large pieces. Place in a baking dish, drizzle with the olive oil and season generously with salt and cracked black pepper. Bake 20 minutes, or until sweet potato is tender.

2 **Meanwhile, cook the pasta** in a large saucepan of rapidly boiling, salted water until al dente. Drain well.

3 **Drain the oil** from the feta and whisk 3 tablespoons of the oil together with the balsamic vinegar to make a dressing.

4 **Steam asparagus** until bright green and tender. Drain well.

5 **Combine the pasta,** sweet potato, asparagus, rocket, feta, tomatoes and pine nuts in a bowl. Add the dressing and toss gently. Season with freshly ground black pepper and serve.

BAKED SWEET POTATO AND WATERCRESS GNOCCHI

SERVES 6

700 g (1 lb 9 oz) orange sweet potato

300 g (11 oz) desiree potatoes

350 g (12 oz) plain (all-purpose) flour

35 g (1 oz/⅓ cup) grated parmesan cheese

30 g (1 oz/1 cup) watercress leaves, finely chopped

1 garlic clove, crushed

60 g (2 oz) butter

25 g (1 oz/¼ cup) grated parmesan cheese, extra

2 tablespoons chopped parsley

1 **Boil sweet potato** and desiree potatoes in their skin until tender. Drain, and when cool enough to handle, peel and press through a potato ricer or mouli into a bowl.

2 **Add the flour,** grated parmesan, watercress and garlic, and season well. Gently bring together with your hands until a soft dough forms. It is important not to overwork the dough to keep the gnocchi tender. Portion into walnut-size pieces and shape using the back of a fork to create the traditional 'gnocchi' shape.

3 **Melt the butter** in a large roasting tray.

4 **Preheat the grill** (broiler) to medium–high heat.

5 **Cook gnocchi** in a large saucepan of boiling salted water for 2 minutes, or until they rise to the surface. Scoop out with a slotted spoon, draining the water off well. Arrange in the roasting tray, tossing gently in the butter, and grill for 5 minutes, or until lightly golden. Sprinkle with the extra parmesan and chopped parsley and serve immediately.

EGGPLANT, RICOTTA AND PASTA POTS

SERVES 4

200 g (7 oz) straight macaroni

125 ml (4 fl oz/½ cup) light olive oil

1 large eggplant (aubergine), cut lengthways into 1 cm (½ inch) slices

1 small onion, finely chopped

2 garlic cloves, crushed

400 g (14 oz) tin chopped tomatoes

400 g (14 oz) ricotta cheese

80 g (1 cup) coarsely grated parmesan cheese

4 tablespoons shredded basil, plus extra to garnish

1 **Preheat the oven** to 180°C (350°F/ Gas 4). Cook the macaroni in a large saucepan of salted boiling water until al dente. Drain.

2 **Meanwhile, heat 2 tablespoons of oil** in a non-stick frying pan over medium heat. Cook the eggplant in three batches for 2–3 minutes each side, or until golden, adding 2 tablespoons of oil with each batch. Remove and drain well on crumpled paper towels. Add onion and garlic to the frying pan and cook over medium heat for 2–3 minutes, or until just golden. Add the tomato and cook for 5 minutes, or until the sauce is pulpy and most of the liquid has evaporated. Season, then remove from the heat.

3 **Combine ricotta,** parmesan and basil in a large bowl, then mix in the pasta. Line base and sides of four 375 ml (13 fl oz/ 1½ cup) ramekins with eggplant, trimming any overhanging pieces. Top with half the pasta mix, pressing down firmly. Spoon on the tomato sauce, then cover with the remaining pasta mixture. Bake for 10–15 minutes, or until heated through and golden on top. Leave for 5 minutes, then run a knife around the ramekin to loosen. Invert onto plates and garnish with a sprig of basil.

FRITTATA OF ZUCCHINI FLOWERS AND RICOTTA

SERVES 4

2 tablespoons olive oil

1 onion, finely chopped

2 garlic cloves, finely sliced

8 small zucchini (courgettes) with flowers

8 eggs, lightly whisked

7 g (¼ cup) oregano, chopped

35 g (1 oz/⅓ cup) ricotta salata, grated (see Note)

25 g (1 oz/¼ cup) grated parmesan cheese

1 tablespoon shaved parmesan cheese

lemon wedges, to serve

1 **Preheat the oven** to 200°C (400°F/ Gas 6). Heat the oil in an ovenproof 20 cm (8 inch) frying pan and cook the onion and garlic until softened. Arrange zucchini flowers evenly in the pan, and add the egg. Sprinkle oregano, ricotta salata and grated parmesan over the top. Season well with black pepper.

2 **Put the pan in the oven** and cook for about 10 minutes, or until set. Remove from the oven and allow to cool slightly. Top with the shaved parmesan, cut into wedges and serve with a piece of lemon.

Note: Originating in Sicily, ricotta salata is a firm, white rindless cheese with a nutty, sweet, milky flavour. Mild feta cheese can be used as a substitute.

GNOCCHI WITH GORGONZOLA AND SAGE SAUCE

SERVES 4

2 x 500 g (1 lb 2 oz) packets potato gnocchi

60 g (2 oz) butter

2 garlic cloves, crushed

1 medium handful small sage leaves

100 g (4 oz) gorgonzola cheese

150 ml (5 fl oz) cream

100 g (4 oz/1 cup) grated parmesan cheese

1 Preheat the grill to high. Lightly grease four 250 ml (9 fl oz/1 cup) heatproof gratin dishes. Cook the gnocchi in a large saucepan of rapidly boiling salted water according to the packet instructions until al dente. Lift the gnocchi out with a slotted spoon, leave to drain, then divide among the prepared dishes.

2 Melt the butter in a small saucepan over medium heat, add the garlic and sage leaves and cook for a few minutes, or until the leaves start to crisp and the garlic browns a little. Pour the sage butter evenly over the gnocchi in the gratin dishes.

3 Dot small knobs of the gorgonzola evenly among the gnocchi. Pour the cream over the top of each dish and sprinkle with the parmesan. Place the dishes under the grill and cook until the top starts to brown and gnocchi are heated through. Serve with a fresh green salad.

Note: This can also be cooked in a 1 litre (35 fl oz/4 cups) rectangular heatproof ceramic dish or round pie dish.

VEGETABLE SKEWERS WITH BASIL COUSCOUS

SERVES 4

5 thin zucchini (courgettes), cut into
2 cm (¾ in) cubes

5 slender eggplants (aubergine), cut into
2 cm (¾ in) cubes

12 button mushrooms, halved

2 red capsicums (peppers), cut into
1.5 cm cubes

250 g (9 oz) kefalotyri cheese, cut into
2 cm (¾ in) thick pieces

80 ml (3 fl oz/⅓ cup) lemon juice

2 garlic cloves, finely chopped

5 tablespoons finely chopped fresh basil

145 ml (5 fl oz) extra virgin olive oil

185 g (7 oz/1 cup) couscous

1 teaspoon grated lemon zest

1   Soak 12 wooden skewers in water for about 30 minutes to prevent their burning on the grill. Thread alternating pieces of vegetables and kefalotyri, starting and finishing with a piece of capsicum and using two pieces of kefalotyri per skewer. Place in a non-metallic dish which will hold them in one layer.

2   Combine the lemon juice, garlic, 4 tablespoons basil and 125 ml (4 fl oz/½ cup) oil in a non-metallic bowl. Season. Pour two thirds of the marinade over skewers, reserving the remainder. Turn to coat, cover with plastic wrap and marinate for at least 5 minutes.

3   Place couscous, lemon zest and 375 ml (13 fl oz/1½ cups) boiling water in a large heatproof bowl. Stand for 5 minutes, or until all the water has been absorbed. Add the remaining oil and basil, then fluff gently with a fork to separate the grains. Set aside, covered.

4   Heat a chargrill pan or barbecue plate to medium–high. Cook the skewers, brushing often with the leftover marinade, for 4–5 minutes on each side, or until the vegetables are cooked and the cheese browns.

5   Divide the couscous and skewers among serving plates. Season, then drizzle with the reserved marinade to taste. Serve with lemon wedges.

TOFU, SNOW PEA AND MUSHROOM STIR-FRY

SERVES 4

250 g (9 oz/1¼ cups) jasmine rice

60 ml (2 fl oz/¼ cup) peanut oil

600 g (1 lb 5 oz) firm tofu, drained, cut into 2 cm (¾ in) cubes

2 teaspoons sambal oelek or chilli paste

2 garlic cloves, finely chopped

400 g (14 oz) fresh Asian mushrooms, sliced (shiitake, oyster or black fungus)

300 g (11 oz) snow peas (mangetout), trimmed

60 ml (2 fl oz/¼ cup) kecap manis

1 **Bring a large saucepan** of water to the boil. Add the rice and cook for 12 minutes, stirring occasionally. Drain well.

2 **Meanwhile,** heat a wok until very hot. Add 2 tablespoons of the oil and swirl to coat. Stir-fry the tofu in two batches on all sides for 2–3 minutes, or until lightly browned, then transfer to a plate.

3 **Add the remaining oil** to the wok, add the sambal oelek, garlic, mushrooms, snow peas and 1 tablespoon water and stir-fry for 1–2 minutes, or until the vegetables are almost cooked but still crunchy.

4 **Return the tofu** to the wok, add the kecap manis and stir-fry for a minute, or until heated through and combined. Serve immediately with the rice.

ARTICHOKE, OLIVE AND GOAT'S CHEESE PIZZA

SERVES 4

25 cm (10 inch) purchased pizza base

80 ml (3 fl oz/⅓ cup) Italian tomato pasta sauce

150 g (6 oz) marinated artichokes, quartered

70 g (2 oz) pitted Kalamata olives

1 garlic clove, thinly sliced

50 g (2 oz) goat's cheese, crumbled good-quality olive oil, to drizzle

2 tablespoons chopped fresh oregano

1 **Preheat the oven** to 220°C (425°F/Gas 7). Place pizza base on a baking tray, then spread with the tomato pasta sauce. Evenly scatter the artichoke pieces, olives and the garlic over the pasta sauce, then top with the crumbled goat's cheese.

2 **Lightly drizzle** the surface of the pizza with olive oil and bake for 20 minutes, or until golden. Sprinkle with fresh oregano and season with salt and freshly ground black pepper. Cut into wedges and serve.

SERVES 8

1 tablespoon olive oil, plus extra

1 onion, finely chopped

2 x 425 g (15 oz) tins chickpeas, drained and rinsed

125 g (4½ oz/½ cup) roasted cashew paste

1 egg

65 g (2¼ oz/¼ cup) tahini

1 teaspoon ground cumin

1 teaspoon ground turmeric

1 tablespoon lemon juice

1 vegetable stock (bouillon) cube

125 ml (4 fl oz/½ cup) tamari

600 g (1 lb 5 oz/3 cups) cooked brown rice

1 small carrot, grated

40 g (1½ oz/½ cup) fresh wholemeal (whole-wheat) breadcrumbs

300 g (10½ oz) bok choy (pak choy),

CORIANDER AND COCONUT SAMBAL

3 handfuls of coriander (cilantro) leaves

1 garlic clove, chopped

1 small green chilli, seeded and finely chopped

1 teaspoon garam masala

2 tablespoons lime juice

3 tablespoons shredded coconut

1   Heat olive oil in a frying pan. Sauté onion for 2–3 minutes, or until golden. Set aside.

2   Put the chickpeas in a food processor with the cashew paste, egg, tahini, spices, lemon juice, stock cube, 2 table-spoons of the tamari and 2 tablespoons water. Blend until smooth. Transfer to a large bowl and add rice, onion, carrot and breadcrumbs and mix well. Divide into 16 portions and form into patties about 1.5 cm (⅝ inch) thick. Then refrigerate for 30 minutes.

3   Finely chop all the sambal ingredients in a food processor. Chill until ready to use.

4   Heat some olive oil in a large deep frying pan. Add patties in batches and cook over medium heat for 3–4 minutes on each side, or until golden and cooked through. Remove and keep warm.

5   Wipe the pan clean and heat a little more oil. Add the bok choy and toss for 1 minute, or until wilted. Add the remaining tamari and toss. Divide among serving plates and top with two patties. Dollop with the sambal and serve.

INDEX

GREAT TASTES 30 MINUTE MEALS